The Cats of Poets Square

A Memoir in Thirty Feral Cats

———

COURTNEY GUSTAFSON

PENGUIN BOOKS

PENGUIN BOOKS

UK | USA | Canada | Ireland | Australia
India | New Zealand | South Africa

Penguin Books is part of the Penguin Random House group of companies
whose addresses can be found at global.penguinrandomhouse.com

Penguin Random House UK,
One Embassy Gardens, 8 Viaduct Gardens, London SW11 7BW

penguin.co.uk

First published in the United States of America by Crown,
an imprint of the Crown Publishing Group, a division of
Penguin Random House LLC, New York 2025
First published in Great Britain by Fig Tree 2025
Published in Penguin Books 2026
001

Copyright © Courtney Gustafson, 2025

The Cats of Poets Square was originally published as *Poets Square*

The moral right of the author has been asserted

Penguin Random House values and supports copyright.
Copyright fuels creativity, encourages diverse voices, promotes freedom
of expression and supports a vibrant culture. Thank you for purchasing
an authorized edition of this book and for respecting intellectual property
laws by not reproducing, scanning or distributing any part of it by any
means without permission. You are supporting authors and enabling
Penguin Random House to continue to publish books for everyone.
No part of this book may be used or reproduced in any manner for the
purpose of training artificial intelligence technologies or systems. In accordance
with Article 4(3) of the DSM Directive 2019/790, Penguin Random House
expressly reserves this work from the text and data mining exception

Typeset by Six Red Marbles UK, Thetford, Norfolk
Printed and bound in Great Britain by Clays Ltd, Elcograf S.p.A.

The authorized representative in the EEA is Penguin Random House Ireland,
Morrison Chambers, 32 Nassau Street, Dublin D02 YH68

A CIP catalogue record for this book is available from the British Library

ISBN: 978–0–241–65075–2

Penguin Random House is committed to a sustainable future
for our business, our readers and our planet. This book is made from
Forest Stewardship Council® certified paper.

Praise for *The Cats of Poets Square*

'Deftly intertwined with the individual stories of all these cats is her own story of how she got there . . . She is clear-eyed about the deviation of her life . . . I read this in two days and loved it' Esther Walker, *The Spike*

'Masterfully weaves together stories of cats with stories of her own life and the lives of her community members – raw, flawed and striving for goodness in a complex world. Her journey from cat observer to dedicated caregiver and community builder is profoundly inspiring' Hannah Shaw, *The New York Times* bestselling author of *Cats of the World*

'In its euphoric kindness and tender suffering, this is an addictive book' Jay Griffiths, author of *Wild*

'Cats are mystical beings, bridging the spiritual and the tangible. *The Cats of Poet Square* is a book that helps us connect to this spiritual world, offering a bridge to the ethereal' Ai Weiwei

'An illuminating and heart-warming read that lays testament to the fact that kindness does indeed rule' *Buzz Magazine*

'A warm memoir about loneliness, love and . . . connection . . . affecting testimony to the need for caring' *Kirkus Review*

'One need not be a cat person to be enchanted by this' *Publishers Weekly*

'[A] poignant, beautifully written debut memoir' *BookPage*

'A story about care and compassion and acts of kindness big and small' Chloë Ashby, author of *Wet Paint*

'Courtney Gustafson writes with uncommon grace about the castoff, the abandoned, the invisible' Lauren Slater, author of *Blue Dreams*

ABOUT THE AUTHOR

Courtney Gustafson is a cat rescuer, community organizer and creator of @poetssquarecats on Instagram and TikTok. She lives and works in Tucson, Arizona.

for Monkey

The difference between *wild* and *feral* may seem subtle, but it's a distinction that matters. A wild animal has evolved that way; everything about it is programmed to survive without interference from people. A feral animal is not the same. Feral animals are those whose species were, at some point, domesticated by people, and then for whatever reason left to survive on their own. Feral animals—their histories, their futures, their survival—are inextricably linked to humankind. Their lives are tied to ours.

Feral, for all the wildness it implies, just means that an animal was abandoned by the system that created it.

Contents

Poets Square
1

My Tiny Tender Heart
19

Hunger
35

Men Call Cats Sluts
49

Sad Boy and Lola
65

Bubbles
87

Mothering
109

Viral Cat Videos and the American Dream
129

In This One the Cats Don't Survive
147

Trash
163

Letting Myself Go
183

The Hotdog Man
199

The Pigeon House
217

An Incomplete List of Names I've Given Cats
237

Acknowledgments
239

The Cats of Poets Square

Poets Square

I moved in first, to the little brick house in Poets Square. Tim had a few weeks left in his lease and he was still packing his stuff, going through all his closets, scrubbing everything thoroughly enough to get his security deposit back. I had already abandoned my old place. My whole life had opened up to all the possibilities of our new house, our little rental, a place we had chosen together. I was ready for a wholly new kind of life.

I was sleeping on a bare mattress in what would become our bedroom. I was imagining all of it: the art we would hang on the walls, the speakers we would set up in the living room, the music we would keep on in the background. The way we would hide here, me and Tim, from everything happening in the world. It was a quiet neighborhood. No problems could reach us.

That first night in the new house I sat alone in the empty living room, every small sound echoing. The TV wasn't set up yet; the internet wasn't working. I spent the evening just listening, learning the noises of the neighborhood. There was a sound at the door that could have been the wind. A sound in the backyard. What sounded like footsteps on the roof.

I kept peering outside—was that the door rattling? a tap on the window?—but I couldn't see anything. I might have thought I was imagining it, except my dog, Maggie, heard it too: her ears were swiveling again and again toward the scuttling sounds across the bedroom ceiling. I stayed up all night that first night, hearing the thumps against the trash cans in the driveway, watching the motion-activated floodlights flash on again and again. Every time there was no sign of anyone around.

The next morning—my first morning there, in the new house—I got up early and went outside, newly brave in the daylight, and the evidence was everywhere. Across the front step, the roof, the driveway: tiny pawprints.

———

BEFORE WE MOVED IN TOGETHER, Tim lived ten minutes away from me, in downtown Tucson, in an apartment building with a safe gated courtyard and a few stray cats always milling about. We had a favorite of the cats: a big brown one we called Mushroom Risotto. *You can name a cat anything*, Tim told me, and this had never occurred to me before. I would have agonized over a name, anxious to get it right. Tim could walk outside in the dark and see a stray cat and instantly name it after whatever we had eaten for dinner.

That was the summer the mountains were on fire. We could smell it from anywhere in the city, the low lingering smoke. The pandemic had begun and Tim and I were alone in our bubble, alone in our new relationship. I was spending every night at his apartment and from his building's balcony we could see all of it: the ambulances screaming toward the hospital, the protesters outside the police station, the flames eating up the mountains. The cats ambling about the bushes below us, their occasional howls late at night.

That summer felt both fraught and easy, watching the world's problems but feeling far away from them. The fires cutting through the forest—what could we do to stop them? I went to work and wore my mask and shielded myself from the smoke, and focused so singularly on myself, on Tim, on what my life could look like in our burgeoning relationship. I would have considered myself a good person then. I wasn't the one who had set the mountains on fire. I spent every evening on Tim's couch, watching him cook for me, savoring the safety of his gated building, his warm meals, his attention. Every night Tim would walk me back to my car and we would kiss in the dark and look for Mushroom Risotto, the cat, his wispy fluff disappearing into the dark. It was the first time in my tiny life that it felt like the world could end, and instead of doing anything about it, I was busy falling in love.

IN DAYLIGHT I FOLLOWED THE PAWPRINTS around the house, trying to figure out where a cat might have come from or gone, but there were too many prints to make sense of. I didn't mention it to Tim, even after a few weeks had passed and he was sleeping in our new bedroom with me. Every night I could hear the cat—two cats? maybe three cats?—prancing across the roof, leaping from the fence, scurrying across the driveway.

I was always worried about ruining things. It was the first time in years it had felt like anything in my life had gone correctly, the first time I felt like I might get the chance to climb into bed and feel cozy and safe, with no cares, no responsibilities, nothing owed to anyone. It was probably just a neighbor's cat.

The new neighborhood was quieter than my old one, and darker—there were no streetlights—and from the backyard I could see the stars better than in any other place I had lived. Every night after Tim went to bed I snuck outside in the dark and stood silently and stared at all the constellations stretched above me. I knew that I was waiting in the dark for something other than stars. If I stood still long enough, I would see them: the sets of glowing eyes, the rustling of a tail disappearing into the bushes. There were more than three cats. The movement along the roof, the dark shapes along the edges of the yard. In the dark we would regard each other, me and those infinite pairs of eyes.

———

HAVE YOU NOTICED, TIM SAID one morning, making coffee in our new kitchen, *that there's always a few cats around?*

Yes, I said. *A few.*

The first cat I saw in daylight was gray and white, skinny and long-legged, and sound asleep on the hood of my car when I went outside to leave for work. *Excuse me*, I whispered to the cat, and when I jingled my keys his yellow eyes flashed open and he panicked, raising his back the way cats do, and ran. That night there was a black cat sitting on our front step when I got home. The next morning there was a fluffy orange tail disappearing into the bushes in our backyard, and a calico cat perched on the fence. Tim was still hauling boxes inside; we were still unwrapping mugs in the kitchen for morning coffee.

Oh yeah, he said, when I told him about the calico. *I saw that one this morning.* He pushed the blinds aside and peered out. *Oh*, he said. *Not that one.*

Sometimes I swear I could look out the window and see a single black cat sitting there, like an omen, and a moment later look again and see a white cat in his place. It felt like every time I blinked there was a new cat outside our house, like they were coming from a portal. I would go outside to check the mail and look up at the sky and see an enormous cat perched at the top of our tree, peering down at me. I would open the back door and come face-to-face with a slinky Siamese, her brown points like knee-high boots, her blue eyes completely crossed. It felt like we were on a prank show, like someone was waiting to see how many different cats they could leave in our driveway before we finally went insane.

I started taking notes, cataloging each cat. *The white cat you saw this morning*, I would ask Tim when we talked on the phone during lunch breaks, *was it short-haired or long-haired?* I had a little notebook, and I was cross-checking my notes. *Long-haired*, he would say, *and not fully white. It had some orange on its tail.*

That was a new one. I made a note.

Where are they coming from? Tim asked. *Where do they hide?* We had toured the house before we moved in and there hadn't been any cats. In daylight they were still barely around. We asked our landlord, introduced ourselves to our new neighbors just to ask if they knew anything about the cats. I was a little afraid they'd say no, that maybe I was making it up. The landlord thought the cats might belong to a neighbor; she remembered there might have been strays in the area. *Oh yeah,* all the neighbors said, waving me away. *There's a few stray cats around.*

TIM WAS MAKING A LOT of risotto those days, when we first moved in together. He loved cooking, and especially loved cooking one recipe again and again, homing in on the flavors, making small adjustments. My unrefined palate could never taste the differences, but Tim would nod or smack his lips, savoring each bite, understanding how incrementally he was making improvements. I envied Tim: how devoted he could be, how precise.

Nearly every night Tim would cook a big pot, leaning over the heat and stirring endlessly, while I lounged on the couch or puttered around the kitchen. I didn't cook. It had always felt like a great failing of mine, that I could barely feed myself. It had been a while since I had felt cared for, and I sank into the feeling. I had spent years living in survival mode, living alone, and I was exhausted by it, with nothing left of me to care for anyone else.

And then suddenly there were these daily steaming bowls of buttery rice, cooked down to broth, the nutty mushrooms, the cheese Tim grated on top. The cozy house we suddenly shared. The cats outside. We had started bickering about them, just a little. I was worried about the cats, every one of them, even the ones I hadn't even seen yet. There were at least a dozen of them from my latest count. How long had they all been surviving out there? Was I supposed to be feeding them? I was trying consciously not to assign them names, not to attach my heart to theirs.

By then it was September and the fire in the mountains was out, quenched down to a smoldering scar across the horizon. I could see it from our backyard, the burn scar, the stretch of red fire retardant dropped from helicopters. *See?* I would think, tucking myself into the bed we newly shared. *They didn't need my help to put out a fire.* If I ignored anything long enough someone else would fix it.

All the cats clamoring outside: they didn't need me. I was almost convinced.

GROWING UP I LOVED CATS so much that I often pretended to be one; long past the age it stopped being cute I was still crawling around on all fours, refusing to eat breakfast unless my parents poured my cereal in a cat bowl and put it on the floor for me. We had a cat—a grumpy calico whose fur was always inexplicably greasy—and although she barely let me touch her, I found her endearing, nearly magical, the way she was this weird little creature who just lived with us, and all she did was sit and hiss. The wood-paneled walls of my childhood bedroom were lined with glossy posters of puppies and kittens, butterflies landing on their noses, baby animals tumbling out of baskets and posing in gardens.

I loved animals. I was a cat person.

What I had never understood, even as an adult who occasionally volunteered to walk dogs at the local shelter, was the actual animality of real animals, the wildness of them. Their biology. The way they give birth and the way they die, the way they reproduce, the things they resort to in order to survive.

Cats had always been all comfort to me: they were soft creatures who lived gentle lives inside our homes, curled by a fireplace, kneading a fleece blanket, sleepy and content. I had never considered—had never had reason to consider—what would happen to cats if you put them outside and left them there, allowed them to revert to their wildness, allowed all their brutal biologies to take over.

I didn't know how to love animals this way.

My only experience with dead cats—with death at all, really—was that childhood calico, who lived to age fifteen and then passed painlessly in my mom's arms at the vet. I was there; I stayed in the room for it. I had felt valiant, staying when the vet offered me the choice to leave, like I could say now that I had witnessed death.

But I had witnessed it with stainless steel and a euthanasia needle, the gift of a painless end to a long life. A cat who had never been without people, not for a single day in her fifteen-year life.

The cats outside the house in Poets Square didn't have people. They didn't seem to want people. They were feral; they ran from us. They hid and hissed, scattered every time we opened the door. They seemed to be a different species from what I thought of as cats; they may as well have been a family of raccoons for all the time they spent digging in our trash and then running away, galloping through the dark, dragging their little paws across our rafters.

Tim had grown up in a trailer on a rural tract of land, in 4-H club, handling animals in all their realities. The husbandry. The gross parts. He understood before I did what would happen with the cats at our house: how they would reproduce, how they would die, how powerless we would be to do much about it. *Are they eating birds?* I would ask him. *Are there mice here?* I didn't understand how they were surviving. I didn't understand that they weren't.

Tim had had barn cats, local strays. It was an accepted reality in his childhood that sometimes a cat would show up and have kittens and sometimes the kittens wouldn't make it. *Oh my god*, I was always saying, thinking of all the things I had never had to consider about cats. It was dusk and we were watching a few of the cats prowl the perimeter of the yard. I hadn't even thought about kittens. Were there kittens somewhere? Were there tiny pawprints I had missed?

Tim shrugged. He said: *They're okay. They've survived this long without you.*

THE CATS WERE ALSO A NUISANCE. I already had a dog—Maggie, my sweet, clumsy boxer mix—and we had chosen to rent the house in Poets Square in part for its fenced-in yard, its grassy patches where she could rest in the shade. Maggie, I learned right away, saw the cats as prey. I had to check the backyard before I could let her out, and the cats would scramble up to safety along the wall, taunting her, just out of reach. Sometimes the cats would claw at the welcome mat outside our front door and the noise would drive Maggie crazy; she would tilt her head back and forth, staring at the door, and whine. All night she would stare at the ceiling where she could hear the cats running across it.

I was worried that Maggie would accidentally hurt a cat, or that I would. Each morning, Tim and I would thump our fists on the hoods of our cars and a cat—a different one each day—would come skittering out of the engine before we started it. I started inspecting the whole driveway before leaving for work, getting out of my car again and again to triple-check that no cats were behind my tires. The cats were digging in the garden, scratching at the roof, peeing in the yard. Maggie went wild every morning with the smells. By then I had counted thirty cats.

I googled it once—*feral cats on my roof, what to do*—and got an ad for a pest control company.

Fast, discrete abatement of cat issues, the ad said. It didn't specify what they would do to the cats. I closed the screen quickly, feeling shame creeping over my shoulders. I went outside and I apologized to the night air, hoping all the cats hiding in the eaves could sense it.

Despite the annoyances of the cats, there was never any question that I would love them. The scruffy calico who always hissed when I walked by, the new white cat that had shown up one night, his eyes dark and wide, the way he stared at me from around the corner and then fled.

There was a little orange cat who sometimes followed me when I walked to the mailbox, and an enormous orange cat who was always gazing serenely at me from the edge of the roof. There was a tiny brown tabby with solemn green eyes who would sit outside our door looking anxious.

Some of the cats looked identical; I thought there was just one gray and white cat until I saw two of them together, and then three, and then four. I couldn't touch any of the cats; most of them ran and hid when I walked outside. Instead, I watched them through the glass like they were zoo animals. More and more I would find myself staring from our kitchen window as the cats existed outside: I was observing them, cataloging them, eyeing them almost suspiciously. Daring them to demand something from me.

And then one day I was in the kitchen, and Tim texted me from the driveway.

Babe, his text said. *I'm petting a cat.*

He was. It was a cat we would eventually name Beebs, which was short for BeeBee, which was short for Belinda. It was a nonsense name, one we pulled from nowhere later that night, as if once we had touched a cat we owed it an identity. Beebs was friendly and stripey and gray, and that night I watched from the window as Tim crouched near the street in his work overalls and she rubbed her head hard against his hand.

That's how it started.

AFTER BEEBS, WE NAMED ONE of the cats Monkey. She was the hissing calico with dark blotches of black and orange across her body. After Monkey we named her sister—another calico, but her inverse: mostly white, just bits of black and orange along her tail. We named her Reverse Monkey.

On my list of cats, I started noting names alongside descriptions, trying to identify each one, learning to distinguish between each of the seven white cats with blue eyes, the three different calicos, the two orange cats, and the many brown tabbies.

It was dangerous to name the cats and I knew it. Being able to tell them apart meant that I could tell when one went missing. Before, they had been just a large mass of cats, an ever-changing rotation of random animals appearing in our driveway, but now that I knew them, I could recognize them, and right away I knew it would consume me. Every morning I watched for BeeBee, for Monkey, for Reverse Monkey. For the cats we named Stephanie and Rihanna and Georgie and Alien, Mr. Business and Dr. Big Butt and Sad Mouth Sam. Muppet and Mini and Sad Boy and Mama, Potato and Possum and Hambone.

They had such silly names and they were such serious cats. Sam was the Siamese cat, cross-eyed with a deformed mouth, always staring solemnly at me from under our neighbor's car. Stephanie was long-haired and black, often sitting on our front step and sneezing, snot crusting around her nose. Hambone had small wounds across his back and was the most terrified cat I had ever seen, always quivering, afraid of his own whiskers when they shook.

Reverse Monkey was a tiny, timid thing. She had started to realize that we lived there, started to understand our routines, and she would wait outside the door for me and then startle when I opened it. Her eyes were big and yellow and blinking, curious, tinged with fear. She had an infection in one eye that left it chronically red-rimmed and watery, the goop from it staining her tiny white face. I had started taking my tea outside every morning, sipping it in the driveway, while Reverse Monkey stared at me from twenty feet away and then ten feet away and then just a few feet away, eyeing me suspiciously, like I might lunge at her.

If it had been just her in the driveway—if we had found not thirty cats living at the house but just one, just Reverse Monkey—I would have known what to do. As a kid I had fed several stray cats that had shown up crying at our front door; I understood that it was the right thing to do. A skinny cat shows up on your doorstep and you open the door to them. But something about the mathematics of it—how to take that one correct thing and multiply it by thirty—stumped me. There were facts of the situation that just didn't add up: I loved cats. I wanted to help them. There were thirty of them. I couldn't let thirty cats into my house.

I couldn't really even feed them. Our lease specified that we weren't allowed to feed any animals outside—it was unclear if our landlord had included this because of the cats—and as simple as it sounds now to argue or ignore, housing was a hard thing to jeopardize. It was mid-pandemic, with apartments rarely available and rents skyrocketing. People were becoming homeless every day, losing their jobs, catching Covid on the streets. Cat food was expensive, and cat food for thirty cats wasn't an option with my budget. There were a few times I wandered the pet food aisle at Walmart, adding up prices in my head, giving up. Thinking about Reverse Monkey in our driveway, thinking about all the skinny cats that would circle our cars. Thinking: *Maybe if I had more money, I could be a better person.*

———

THERE WERE SO MANY SWEET THINGS about that house in Poets Square. Our landlord had raised her son there and we could still see the marks on the kitchen doorframe where she had measured his height as he grew. The bedroom was still painted a childish green, the ceiling still covered in glow-in-the-dark stars. How badly I wanted my life to be full of sweetness, full of care. I wanted to bask in it. The way Tim cooked for me, the warm smell of pancakes when I woke up in the morning. I had never been a hopeful person and I had never felt worse about the world, all the things going wrong in it, all the things I couldn't fix. The pandemic raged on and people we knew were dying. My family lived on the other side of the country. My job, my cold empty sanitized office, felt bleak.

Outside, all night, the cats would yowl.

We would eat dinner on the couch and hear a cat wailing outside and I would run to it. I would stop anything we were doing for the cats. I had started getting a sick feeling in my stomach all the time, and it could only be stopped when I went outside and sat crosslegged on the ground in the driveway as the cats moved silently around me, trying to keep all of them in my sight. Watching their dark shapes move along the roof, their glowing eyes blinking from the trees.

I started making daily head counts, daily rounds, needing constant reassurance that all the cats were okay. I scattered small handfuls of cat food in our carport, secretly, hoping the landlord wouldn't notice. I put a bowl of fresh water near the fence. I left a single folded blanket just outside our door: my small offering to whichever cat would choose it.

I cried a lot. *I know I can't save them all*, I told Tim. *I just don't want to see them suffer.*

That had felt like a noble thing to say. It would be a year before I would start to think about the difference between *I don't want them to suffer* and *I don't want to SEE them suffer*, how easily I had felt like a good person before the suffering was right outside my door. Before I was forced to face it.

Reverse Monkey had claimed the blanket by the door and every morning I would find her there, curled against the cold, looking up at me like she was pleading, willing me to understand something I couldn't. I didn't know that she was pregnant.

The cats would howl all night and show up hurt in the morning, newly limping and bloodied, their faces torn up. Their coats were dull; their ribs were showing. There were so many of them, and every day I looked out at them and felt something like shame, a hot hollow guilt I didn't know what to do with, like that specific childhood shame of winning a goldfish at the state fair and finding it belly up the next day, like I had failed a living creature without ever having had a chance to know better.

———

I STARTED HAVING DREAMS ABOUT Mushroom Risotto, the cat from Tim's old courtyard. It had felt frivolous to name him, to say hi to him every night. Had he belonged to anyone? Was he lost? He used to meow curiously as we kissed in the dark outside Tim's old apartment, saying goodbye until we saw each other the next day. We had been counting down the days until we wouldn't have to leave each other every night, until we'd wake up in the same house every morning. *Goodnight, Mushroom Risotto*, we'd say to the cat, and he'd dart just out of reach, looking at us simultaneously scared and wanting. Was he a stray? Were there more of him? I had taken his existence at face value, as fact. I had never once thought to feed him.

In Poets Square I kept wondering what the people who lived there before us had done about the cats, why no one else seemed to have helped them, why the neighbors had waved me away. *There's a few stray cats around*, they had said.

The house had a covered carport, and instead of parking either of our cars there we saved the space for the cats. When it rained—thick, drenching monsoon storms—the cats would convene in the carport, all of them trying to stay dry. *There's a bunch of soggy cats out there*, Tim would say, and after the storm I would go outside with dry towels and cat treats. I started leaving more and more things there—little cat beds, a few toys—and every morning the first thing I did was check on the cats in the carport. The beds would be covered in cat hair, the treats long since eaten.

I wanted to love the cats the way I understood how to: with silly names and cute toys, a few treats, warm blankets. The cats still hissed and ran, refused to descend from the roof. The cats swarmed the small amounts of food I could afford. They ignored the toys; they didn't know how to play. They didn't know their names. They were mating, I realized, when they howled and cried all night. They were making more of themselves. They were getting hurt. They were dying.

I was thinking of my childhood calico, how I had been there when she died. How this was nothing like that at all.

The cats were dying slowly, sick and starving, and they were dying suddenly, in the streets, as cars sped by. They were dying before they were even born, and that's my most visceral memory of those early months at the new house: walking outside one morning in the cold and seeing Reverse Monkey huddled in a corner, her body heaving, her kittens already dead.

I had loved animals all my life. *What a dream*, people would say to me, when I told them I had accidentally moved into a house that came with thirty feral cats.

You're so lucky, people would say. *I love cats.*

I loved cats but I had never loved cats like this: at their wildest, their most brutal, the way nature had overtaken them and left only suffering, only starvation and death. When I picked up Reverse Monkey's dead kittens I tucked them safely in a box with a blanket, the way I would have if they had been alive, and surveyed the driveway like it was the aftermath of a battle. Tim's words were repeating in my mind: *They've survived this long without you.*

My Tiny Tender Heart

I started an Instagram account for the cats because it felt like a way to care about them. For cats who seemed to have been ignored and unloved for so long, it felt like it meant something to love them publicly.

I was scraping together enough money to buy cat food in bulk, trying to ration it to the skinniest cats, having absolutely no idea how I'd ever afford vet care, all of it overwhelming and impossible. But here was something I could do: I could give the cats names, and learn their little personalities, and take cute pictures of them. I could post them online. I could let other people love them, too.

To be honest, I started the Instagram account primarily for my dad, who lived on the other side of the country and with whom I communicated almost exclusively through pictures of our pets. He had been cataloging the cats at Poets Square along with me: I would send him pictures and he would guess at their names, trying to learn all thirty. *That's BeeBee, right?* he would say, to a picture of Trader

Joe. *I know this one*, he'd say, to a picture of Goldie. *That's definitely Dr. Big Butt.*

My dad had always loved cats and had recently lost his own. He was constantly talking about adopting a new companion, and avoiding big topics like the pandemic and the election and the way the world could ruin both of our lives at any moment. Now here was a thing we could connect over: pictures of cats.

GOLDIE WAS THE FIRST CAT to make me cry in a good way, to cry because I hadn't known I could feel so strongly about a creature.

We called Goldie the tiny king of Poets Square. He was a royal boy, the way he pranced through the front yard, marching up to visitors like they needed his permission to be there. The whole neighborhood knew him: the skinny orange cat with the impossibly long tail. Goldie was friendly and completely unafraid. He would run up to strangers, sniff dogs walking by the house, climb to the very top of our trees. He trusted me before he had any reason to.

My heart attached itself almost unwillingly to Goldie; I didn't have a choice. When I stood outside, he would climb my body like a tree, insisting on settling himself into my arms whether or not I bent down to pick him up. He was a raggedly little cat with leaky eyes and a dull coat, dirty paws and a kink in his tail. He was too skinny. When he weaved himself between my feet, I could see the way his body tucked in by his hips; I could see his ribs. He was always scratching his ears, always flicking his head, always struggling to eat with his crooked little mouth. He was a mess of a cat, but unbothered by any of it. I would sit with him and he would purr, and my body would settle into his purring.

I hadn't considered my heart to be brittle before then but suddenly it felt softer, the way Goldie would let me rake my fingers through his fur, the way later in the day I would look outside and see him sleeping, his fur still showing the pattern of how I had pet him. He was so skinny that when he slept on his side, he looked flat, fully collapsed, but there it was in dusty orange fur: the imprint of my own hands.

I WAS CONSTANTLY SHOWING cat pictures to everyone I knew. I had become obsessed with the cats; I couldn't help it. I would show Tim a picture of Goldie, and then another picture of Goldie, and then another. *Here he is sleeping,* I would say. *Here he is eating. Look how cute! Here he is sleeping again.*

Babe, Tim would say gently, as I swiped to another picture of the same skinny orange cat. *I know what Goldie looks like. I can see him right now.* And he would gesture out the window at the driveway, where Goldie was sitting, skinny and orange, staring in at us.

I could feel myself becoming softer: more tender, more obsessed. Each day I raced home to stare at the cats outside our window. The rest of my life had mostly stayed the same; I got up every morning and went to work, and ran my errands, and went to the gym, and the whole time I was thinking: *They don't know I have thirty cats now.*

GOLDIE WAS THE MASCOT for the whole group—all the more skittish cats that would keep their distance from me, the feral pair who lived on the roof, the most scared of them who would only appear for meals after dark, after I had gone inside. The cats who were unsure, watching me warily from a distance, approaching only after I sat very still for hours, treats balanced on my outstretched palms. Goldie was their ambassador, the one who would press his nose against the kitchen window until I brought food outside for all of them. *Don't forget about us*, he would seem to say, his eyes widening when he saw me come into view.

When I started the Instagram account for the cats it was Goldie—his tiny, triangular face—that I chose as the profile picture.

IT WAS LIKE A REALITY SHOW, the way some of the cats who had been fighting were suddenly friends, the way I would realize one day that one cat was another cat's mother. There was a clear patriarch of the group—Sad Boy—and he had a clear female mate, and sometimes the other female cats would try to oust her, try to move in on Sad Boy.

And no one watches a reality show just for the content; you watch it so that afterward you can gossip about it, text your friends who are also watching to talk about the big twist at the end of this week's episode. I would ask Tim if he had seen that Stephanie, the black cat, was now hanging out with Dr. Big Butt, the huge orange one. *Monkey is playing!* I would text him. *With Rihanna! Lola is in the driveway. She's hissing at everyone but François doesn't seem to care. MK is watching from the roof. There's a new Siamese cat?? Haven't seen Christian Dior but he's probably next door.*

Tim tried very hard to care. He liked the cats, always stopped in the driveway to rub his hand over the little heads of whoever was around, but he had not become enamored by their antics the way I had. He wasn't keeping up with the reality show. I felt like I was watching a program no one else had access to, and I needed someone to understand. I wanted to share a photo on Instagram and get the response I was looking for: *Is that BeeBee and Mr. Business? Sharing a bed??*

GOLDIE FELT LIKE HE WEIGHED NOTHING. I could scoop him up with one hand, hold him under my arm like a football. Sometimes he seemed to have no bones; he could contort himself in my lap into a pretzel, a twisted ball of skinny orange limbs. I'd find him sleeping in one of the beds I had started leaving in the driveway, tucked away so soundly that I couldn't tell which end his head would pop up from when I tapped him. *Goldie*, I'd whisper, knowing he wouldn't wake up. Sometimes I worried he was deaf. Sometimes I worried that I had accidentally turned my entire heart into a tiny orange cat, and now it was running around the streets, trying to survive.

GOLDIE SEEMED TO LIKE THE IDEA of food, but not the reality of eating. He would come running when he heard the sound of kibble filling a bowl, or when he smelled the tuna-flavored treats I shook to entice him. He was so desperately skinny and I didn't know what to do about it. His mouth was crooked, his teeth didn't quite line up, and I wondered if it hurt him to chew. I started buying soft food for him, and then soft treats, and a whole variety of cat soups and purees. I had stopped making student loan payments and was spending the money on cat food instead.

There was a product called Lil' Gravies that came in colorful pouches and for a while those pouches were always all over our house, all the different flavors I tried to tempt Goldie with. I bought a tube of high-calorie cat gel, which I hadn't previously known existed, and coaxed him to lick a bit off my finger.

He only ate if I was hand-feeding him. If I put food down and went inside, the other cats would slurp it noisily, but Goldie would instantly lose interest and wander away. If another cat tried to eat from his bowl, he would let them. Many of the other cats would fight each other, hiss at each other, tumble and yowl together through the yard, but Goldie seemed to be exempt from any of this; the other cats either loved him or paid him no mind.

I spent a lot of time feeling like a mad scientist in my kitchen, mixing soft foods with water and mashing them into a soup, mixing cat purees and cat gels and all the flavors of Lil' Gravies. Anything to get Goldie to eat. He liked to sit sphinxlike under the truck in our driveway and I would army-crawl under there with him, on my belly, pulling myself forward with my elbows. How many times the neighbors must have seen just my legs sticking out from under that truck. All because this tiny orange cat I had never meant to love would only lick his carefully concocted bowl of calories if I was right there with him, my face inches from his. He would eat a few licks, his tongue barely dipping into the bowl, and then instead of eating he would touch his nose to mine and we would stay like that: my forehead pressed to his tiny orange one, me whispering to him as we lay under the truck on the grease-stained driveway.

I shared all of this on Instagram, and I never questioned why. It felt like the most I had ever cared for another creature, the greatest lengths I had gone to keep someone alive. Afterward it felt like maybe I was just bragging. Haven't plenty of people fed a stray cat in their driveway without posting it online for praise? Did I need strangers on the internet to tell me that crawling under a truck each day made me good?

It would be years before I really considered what my motivations had been and tried it on to see if it felt true: *I started an Instagram account for the cats because I wanted people to think I'm good.*

———

GOLDIE STILL SPENT HIS TIME in the street, dodging cars in the dark. By then I had filled our covered carport with cat trees and beds, cardboard scratchers and little fabric cubes the cats could hide in, all donated from strangers who followed the cats on Instagram. He had plenty of safe spots to sleep, plenty of toys to keep him busy, but he was mischievous and full of energy: he would scamper across the street to the bushes where the lizards hid, chase snakes down the driveway, somehow get stuck on the roof.

I loved how brave Goldie was around me; I found myself getting annoyed with the other cats for the way they ran from me. *You know me*, I would tell them, as they scattered. *I'm the person who gives you treats each night.* I would toss a treat toward François and he would flinch, his ears going flat. He'd sniff it like it might be a trick, eye me suspiciously. When the cats gathered around me for food I had to sit perfectly still; the slightest movement would send them all terrified and running. Once, crouched quietly in the carport with all the cats, I suddenly had to sneeze. It was like a bomb had been dropped, the way the cats fled. They never came back out that night and regarded me warily the next morning.

Goldie didn't make me work for his trust. He loved me instantly and automatically, the way he would have loved anyone who had moved into that house. I took it as a sign, tried to make it mean something, the way Goldie would let out squeaky little meows until I sat down for him, until I let him settle into my lap. I couldn't quite understand who I was becoming with Goldie, how the cats had changed the pace of my life. How crucial it had become for me to pause and sit outside with a tiny orange cat. How soft I felt alongside him.

But Goldie loved everything; he loved indiscriminately. He was infinitely curious: he'd paw at a wasp nest, explore the whole neighborhood, approach moving vehicles like they might be driving by specifically to say hi to him. He was a dangerous cat to attach myself to, and I was staying up later and later each night to supervise him. I'd get in bed and feel my heart pounding with worry, my fears all wrapped up in a cat who was trying to get himself killed. The next morning I would run to the window and make sure he was there, asleep in the driveway, before I could do anything else. Sometimes he had little scratches on him, or leaves stuck in his fur: all the evidence of whatever mischief he had gotten into in the night. My heart was so breakable. I had never felt so fragile.

IT WAS IMPOSSIBLE NOT TO feel joy watching the cats. A friend sent a package of cat toys his own cat had rejected, and I spread them out over the driveway: colorful balls and mice, plastic springs, little ribbons and bells. The cats gathered around the toys, marveled at them. I had never felt anything like it in my life, whatever emotion it was to watch a ragtag group of misfit strays try cat toys for the first time in their lives.

Reverse Monkey reached a paw out, tentative, toward a stuffed orange ball. François was watching, fascinated. Goldie trotted over—never tentative about anything—and dove in, running wildly between the toys, pawing at them and pouncing on them, and then it was a frenzy, so many of the cats jumping in to play. To really play, with real toys, for the first time.

———

AND THEN ONE MORNING GOLDIE wasn't in his bed. He wasn't in the driveway. He wasn't dead in the street—I checked—but he also wasn't on the roof or in the trees or under the truck, waiting for his two bites of breakfast, his daily ritual of pressing his head against mine.

Three days went by with no sign of Goldie. We searched. I sobbed, feeling my sadness creeping into my knees, across my collarbones, into my spine. I was racked by it. Tim was solemn. The other cats were the same as the day before: still waiting for food, still taking over our driveway in moving masses of black and gray and white. I looked out the window every minute for orange.

When Goldie returned, it was dark out. Tim saw him first. *Babe!* he shouted into the house. I had never heard his voice sound so urgent. *He's here. He's hurt.*

He was. Goldie had big wounds across his neck and his shoulder. He was bleeding. His jaw was more crooked than usual. I put a bowl of food in front of him and his mouth was moving wrong; he was nearly choking on his own tongue. His jaw was broken. He seemed scared all of a sudden, flinching when I pressed a clean cloth to the blood on his neck. I moved my face close to his and he didn't react. *Goldie*, I whispered, and he whimpered back.

I didn't post this on Instagram. None of it.

GOLDIE RECOVERED. IT TOOK a long time. It took vet appointments and ointments and lots of that high-calorie cat gel. He got a bath and ear drops and soft food, careful tending to his wounds, antibiotics.

He got his claws trimmed. He wouldn't need them to be sharp enough to defend himself again.

I was spending all my time googling cat rescues, learning every shelter, every low-cost vet clinic in town. The first time I took Goldie to the vet it smelled like animals and antiseptic, the waiting room too sterile, Goldie stressed and meowing from inside his carrier. I felt like I was doing everything wrong. I was apologizing to Goldie and I was sad. Someone on Instagram had donated the carrier. Someone I didn't even know.

A local rescue took Goldie in. I sobbed the whole way there and I left him hiding and scared in a big crate. I had never seen him scared before, my orange boy, my whole unafraid heart. The night before I drove Goldie away from Poets Square I wore a soft red T-shirt, oversized, nearly to my knees. I planned to send it with him in the morning, something that smelled like me. Instead I spent that night dreaming anxious stress dreams and I woke with the shirt soaked through with sweat, smelling sharp and vinegary. I took the pillowcase off my pillow instead, sniffing it to make sure it smelled like me.

I had never met the woman who would be taking care of Goldie. How strange, to hand off a cat that had begun to feel like my own. For weeks after that I slept without a pillowcase. For weeks I saw my dumb yellowing pillow, all the stains where I had drooled in my sleep, and I looked out the window and did not see Goldie.

He survived, Tim would remind me. *He's safe now. We don't have to chase him out of the street every night.*

I couldn't tell anymore if what I was feeling was sadness or anger. Was it grief? I hadn't asked for this situation. I hadn't asked to inherit thirty cats and then divide up my tiny, tender heart into the bodies of creatures I couldn't save. Goldie was safe. There were still twenty-nine others. They didn't seem to notice he was gone.

———

I STARTED AN INSTAGRAM ACCOUNT for the cats because I needed help. I didn't know it then.

———

PEOPLE FROM INSTAGRAM HAD STARTED sending me money for Goldie's vet bills. I hadn't asked them to. It had never occurred to me that people might help, that I didn't have to save all thirty cats by myself. It was my dad and my aunt and my old friends from college who were sending me money for the cats, but it was also strangers. *You have painted such a vivid picture of these cats in your carport*, people would comment, and I would think: *Who are you? How did you find me?*

Goldie suddenly had fans, and he deserved to. He was staying with a foster, and she sent me pictures of him every night. I remember the one that made me cry: Goldie sitting at the very top of a massive cat tree in front of a picture window, looking out over the desert, watching the birds and the rabbits and the lizards. Safely, from indoors. *He really hates eating*, his foster told me, and I sent her pictures of all the things I had tried. *He likes Lil' Gravies*, I told her, and the next day she sent me a picture of a whole pile of them, the little gravy pouches, and Goldie licking his food in the background. I realized I had loved Goldie so singularly that I hadn't believed anyone else could love him correctly.

I started an Instagram account for the cats because I had too much love for them, scary amounts of weird obsessive love for these creatures in my carport who could, at any moment, just die. I had a creeping sense of how big my grief would become. I was inviting someone to share it with me. *Please*, I was saying. *I cannot feel this much by myself.*

———

GOLDIE'S FOSTER FOLLOWED ME on Instagram. *Oh my god*, she messaged me. *You have thirty more of them?*

She was sending me pictures of Goldie eating treats, Goldie meeting her other cats, Goldie lounging on her couch. Goldie curled up on my old pillowcase. I was still sleeping without one. Tim kept reminding me to go buy a new one, but it felt like some sort of weird punishment not to, something I deserved. I had let Goldie get injured. I had left him there, outdoors, and he was hurt. I would sleep on a bare pillow.

That doesn't make sense, Tim would say.

Goldie gained weight. His wounds healed. He fought off the weird infection in his ears. His eyes were clearing up, he could hear better, he had started to like food. *He eats now!* his foster told me. *I can't believe how much he eats. He's a new cat.*

I spent every night outside in the carport, without Goldie. *What am I gonna do with the rest of you?* I would ask the other cats. They circled me.

I was posting more and more on Instagram, sometimes three or four or five times a day. I was posting Goldie updates, and everyone loved them. I was posting the other cats: the treat time crew that showed up every night, the feral pair that stared down from the roof, the new cats who I would see just once or twice from a distance. People I didn't know were choosing their favorites. People would ask: *Which of the cats is next?*

Caring for the cats was an overwhelming task and I was spending a lot of time crying, a lot of time feeling like my heart was too small and too tender, a lot of time wishing I could disengage, wishing I had not been the one to find these cats. I had barely started helping them—hadn't even meant to—and I already wanted to quit. But it was too late: strangers on Instagram loved them. Strangers were waiting to see what would happen next. Strangers were cheering me on, sending me money, waiting to see how many cats I could save.

GOLDIE'S FACE WAS STILL my profile picture, still the icon I saw every day when I logged in, when he was adopted by a family with a nineteen-year-old son. His new family found me on Instagram. *This is his new dad*, they wrote, with a picture of their son holding Goldie like an infant, like a proud father. They somehow looked alike: that same earnestness, the same bright eyes.

Goldie had become enormous. His coat was thicker, shinier, more orange. I hadn't realized how dull he had looked in my driveway, how sickly, but in the pictures now it was clear: this was the cat Goldie was meant to be. He couldn't have been that cat with me.

I asked for permission to share the photos on Instagram. I put a pillowcase back on my bed.

Thank you for bringing this cat into my life, Goldie's new dad messaged me. *I love him so much. I can't imagine not having him.*

I couldn't imagine it either, not having him. I was still feeling something like grief, or like guilt, something at the edges of my happiness, when I sat surrounded by the cats. I felt it acutely, the stress and concern, the overwhelm of all these animals who had decided I was in charge of them. My handful of followers had implored me to create an online wishlist for the cats, all the kinds of cat food we needed. Suddenly there were packages arriving at the door. Suddenly the cats were eating well, three times a day, and I was watching them turn into something like real cats—their coats getting shinier, their faces filling out.

I wanted to share all of it: my grief and my overwhelm, my anxiety and joy and obsession. The exact frequency of Goldie's purring against my chest, how it calmed me, steadied my breathing. I didn't want any of it to only be mine. That's why I started an Instagram account for the cats: because I didn't want to do any of it alone.

Hunger

When we inherited the cats, I was working at a food bank. My job was marketing and fundraising, writing web content in a little windowless office. But this was during the pandemic: suddenly whole departments of staff were quarantined at home, coworkers were hospitalized, coworkers died. All our operations, all our food distributions, shifted to be outdoors and socially distanced and we were all pitching in to keep things running. I spent half my days portioning meals, packing food boxes, working the food line. Motioning to masked people on the other side of car windows and then wordlessly loading their trunk with nonperishable food.

It became national news, how high the demand at food banks had become. Ours was a huge one: it served the entire bottom half of Arizona, some of the poorest counties in the nation. We had hundreds of families at a time arriving every day for help.

We operated out of a warehouse and from my little office upstairs I could always hear the forklifts under me. I liked to get to work early, before the gates opened to the public and the lines started forming, because I was uncomfortable walking by lines of hungry people to get to my desk. I felt bad about this. I didn't know how else to feel.

It was a desperate time, past those early days of the pandemic when everyone was donating handmade masks and thanking frontline staff, all camaraderie and helping each other out. It was months after that, when lockdowns were dragging on and people were still dying, and the lines for food became so long that the cars were blocking traffic. We had to hire cops to shut down the street and redirect the people whose morning commutes were blocked by people who were just trying to get groceries. There was a lot of honking, a lot of gesturing, a lot of people throwing up their arms behind car windows as if to say: *What do you want me to do?*

Each morning, I would feed the cats and they would scramble for the food, big writhing masses of cats, all trying to get their mouths to the bowl at the same time. They would growl as they ate, reach their paws out and smack each other out of the way. I tried to portion out the food, to put down a bunch of bowls at once, but it didn't matter: the cats were desperate and swarming and every morning I felt the anxiety of it, of trying to make sure they each got enough, of trying to make sure they didn't hurt each other in the midst of all the hissing.

All the plants outside our house were browning, wrinkled, trying to conserve water. Before work I said a daily prayer to the dying aloe in the yard; it wasn't getting what it needed but it was trying. It was August, the temperature in the triple digits every day, the people waiting for food forced to keep their cars running so they didn't overheat like dogs.

WHEN I MET MONKEY I described her as a mean, scheming little gremlin. She had revealed herself right away as the bully of the group, the cat who would eat her food fastest and then sneak up on the other cats to steal theirs. The cat who would smack anyone that got in her way.

Monkey, I was always saying, chastising her. *Let the other cats eat.*

Monkey was a skinny little calico with a head that seemed too small for her body. She was standoffish, prone to biting if I tried to touch her, but she never ran away from me. She always wanted food. She had big goblin eyes and a tendency to narrow them, to squint up at me in a way that made it look like she was smirking. She was so brash about it, the way she'd walk up to another cat and smack them, claws out, until they ran away. The way she'd eat all their food, a low growl keeping the other cats away as she ate, and then sit there. Smirking.

I would sit in the driveway with my plastic tub of treats and dole them out to each cat: one treat for François, one treat for Rihanna, one treat for Sad Mouth Sam. The cats would sit in a big semicircle around me, like we were all at a campfire together, and then Monkey would come barreling through the group, knocking the other cats out of the way like bowling pins. If I offered her a treat she'd hiss and scratch me, trying to get to it faster. Then she'd swallow it whole.

You have to stop doing that, I was always telling her. I mixed up a special meal for Goldie, a tuna-flavored high-calorie gel to put some weight on him, and seconds later found Monkey licking the bowl clean instead. *That wasn't for you*, I told her, and she let out a low grumble, a constant growl she kept ready in her throat. The bowl was empty. She was still licking it, desperately, her goblin eyes bugging out of her head. One paw poised to smack me.

THERE'S NO WAY TO PROVIDE emergency grocery assistance to thousands of people each month and also acknowledge the humanity of each of those people. The logistics don't allow for it. And you might think this is wrong—it shouldn't be about logistics, it should be about people—and you'd be right. But you'd be right in the way that I was when I first started working at the food bank: right in a way that didn't translate in any meaningful way to real life. Naïve. I had so much optimism when I started the job, so bright-eyed about the world, as if I alone had the kind of compassion that could solve systemic food insecurity.

We distributed food mostly through federal programs, which meant we had to follow federal rules. To pick up food, families had to register; they had to self-declare their household income and show a photo ID and prove that they lived within our service area. These steps provided data that was sometimes useful to my work in fundraising—I could send pleading letters to the wealthy parts of town and I could include the exact demographics of the families we served, the number of children they had, how large the gap was between their income and the current cost of food—but sometimes it felt like these steps existed just to add to the shame of it, just to slow down the line. Elderly couples, young moms wrangling toddlers, teenagers on their own—they'd all stand in line filling out paperwork, presenting the little yellow cards that told us they were repeat visitors. *Has your income changed since last month?* we had to ask. *Has there been any change to the number of members in your household?*

Much of the time I spent working at food distributions was not actually spent distributing food. I was mostly there as a member of the marketing team, the person whose job was to witness everything happening and then turn it into an inspiring story for social media. This meant that in the dichotomy between people who needed food and people who were handing out food, I was neither: I was the person skulking around the perimeter with a camera, taking photos of masked volunteers cheerfully loading car after car with canned peas and Cheerios.

But it wasn't really a dichotomy: some of the food bank employees also qualified for food assistance. They never picked it up at these public distributions. It was kind of a secret, which of my coworkers worked for the food bank but were paid too little to buy groceries. I also qualified for food assistance, technically, but I didn't realize it until years later. I wasn't making enough money to pay my bills, especially in all the years before moving in with Tim when I paid the rent alone. But I had a hard time recognizing this; I couldn't reconcile my forty-hour-a-week job, my master's degree, my years of thinking I was doing everything right, with the simple fact that I was struggling. Instead, I felt alien to all of it: the people waiting for hours to reach the front of the line, the people volunteering their mornings to stand in the heat, moving pallets of brown rice and dry beans.

I was buying the cheapest kind of cat food those days, the kind that someone on the internet will tell you will kill your cat. It didn't matter. My budget barely allowed for anything extra, and I spent it all on off-brand cans of liver-flavored paté, scooped it into the cheapest plastic bowls I could find at Walmart. It was never enough for the cats, who licked the bowls clean in seconds and then waited for more. It was never enough for Monkey, who would make sure the other cats didn't get to eat.

I was annoyed with Monkey all the time. *Can you chill?* I would ask her, my tone growing more and more exhausted, meaner and meaner. I was exhausted from work, exhausted from staying up late with the cats, exhausted from watching all the hunger around me. I would physically push Monkey out of the way as the other cats ate, chase her away from the bowls when she'd come back for more. I made no efforts at patience. I would refill her bowl and she'd scratch me, leaving thin trails of blood along my fingers.

Can you just be grateful for what you got? I'd ask her, knowing she had no way to understand this. She'd stare back at me with her giant eyes, unblinking. She was all animal. All hunger.

It's a simple expectation: that if you help someone, they will be grateful for it. That if someone is hungry and you give them food, they should be glad for it. Sometimes it was true. Sometimes at work I would watch a volunteer hand an extra box of granola bars to a kid in the back seat and his mom would put a hand to her heart, mouth *Thank you* through the window. Sometimes a family would be thrilled with how much food they got, and you could see it on their faces: the gratitude, the relief of another month of meals. Sometimes someone would write us a note, a small card with a story about how much they had been struggling, and pass it to a volunteer through a cracked driver's-side window. *God bless all of you. For all the help.*

Those were the stories I would share on social media, in the newsletters that we sent to our top-level donors, in the year-end reports we delivered to the government so they would keep funding the emergency food program.

But the reality was complicated.

I can't eat any of that, a woman would say as volunteers packed her car with cereal and white bread. She was diabetic. She was right. Someone would tell us that they had no teeth and could only eat soft foods, that they were allergic to peanut butter, that they couldn't eat gluten. There was no protocol for this; every time someone rejected food, the volunteers would freeze, their arms still full of packaged loaves of bread, looking helplessly around. A young mother would see that the brand of oatmeal we were handing out had changed that month and she would crumple, trying not to cry. *My kid won't eat that*, she would say. *I know it's all you have. But he won't eat it.*

Some people stared straight ahead. I used to think this was shame, this refusal to make eye contact, but as the pandemic stretched on and the food lines got longer, I realized it was something closer to defeat. People were rude: to us, to each other. They were rude to the volunteers directing traffic, rude to the volunteers lifting gallons of milk into their cars, rude to the staff moving fresh pallets of eggs. They were rude to the other people waiting in the line, the cars idling in front of them for hours, laying on their horns to get someone to inch forward. Sometimes we'd pack a car full of food and the driver would roll down the window just enough to flash us a middle finger and speed away. Sometimes a car had been waiting for hours to pick up the most basic of groceries, just enough to get through a few more days, and they would get to the front of the line and see us there and say: *Honestly, fuck this. Fuck all of you.*

AT WORK WE SOMETIMES GOT free lunch—a stack of pizzas or a catered sandwich platter—and I found myself feeling panicked about it, like if I didn't take enough I might starve, like food was a finite resource and I had to squirrel it away for winter. I was always comparing my plate to everyone else's, wondering how much I could get away with taking, how much I could eat before someone called me out. I was eating late at night, in large amounts, specifically when Tim wasn't awake to see me.

I mentioned it to my therapist with a sense of shame. *I don't know how to explain it*, I told her, *except that I need all of it.*

We were meeting over Zoom and her face kept freezing onscreen.

You're resource guarding, she told me. *Like a dog.*

It was what Monkey was doing, too: the low growl she let out as she ate, the claws that came out if anyone got near her. It looked like aggression, but it was a message: *Please don't take this from me. I need this. Please.*

Sometimes I would look out the window and see Monkey sniffing around the yard at rocks and plants, checking every single thing to see if it was edible.

I talked in therapy about my sense that something was wrong with me, that I was fundamentally flawed on some essential, unfixable level. Sometimes I felt like I wasn't capable of being good in the way that other people were. It was baffling to me, how easily a coworker could offer me the last cookie at lunchtime without feeling like she had to keep it for herself. Sometimes I would collect Post-it notes and water bottles and bowls from the break room, any snacks that were left out, and hide them in my desk. I'd lie if anyone asked if I had them. I told myself that was just my personality: a little selfish, a little prone to bending the truth.

ON INSTAGRAM I KEPT GETTING the same comment, the one thing everyone wanted to know: what did we need most for the cats?

Food, I responded, again and again, watching Monkey out the window. So much cat food. The way she'd stare through the window at me, inching closer to the door, her hunger so immense it radiated from her.

The cat food showed up at our door in cases, in bags of kibble larger than I knew cat food could come in. Fifty-pound bags, sixty-can cases. Beef in gravy, salmon paté, chicken Florentine. Flavors of cat food I didn't know existed. Having a lot of something always made me anxious about losing it. I counted all the cans, measured out the dry food, did the math. Monkey was watching me. We could afford to feast.

It took six months of consistent meals—twice a day, every day, as much as she wanted—for Monkey to stop scaring the other cats away from their food. If I was late with a meal, even by a few minutes, she would regress instantly: back to hissing, back to swatting at my hands to be fed faster.

The physical changes in her came first. The black parts of her fur had been dull, the white parts scruffy, the orange on her face always crusty from plunging her whole face into the food. She was skinny when we found her, a shell of a cat. It happened so slowly that I didn't notice it, and then it felt like it happened overnight: I went outside with breakfast one morning and she was shiny, filled out, her eyes brighter. *Monkey*, I said to her. I was feeling a surge of affection for her, a realization of how desperately she had needed me. *You look good.*

It took longer for her brain to catch up. I wished so many times she could understand me when I told her I would never let her be hungry again. *I will always feed you*, I told her every single night when I gave her dinner. I was certain it was true. I had cat food hidden all over our house; with every new delivery of donated food I stashed some away, hid twelve cans at a time in every drawer and every closet. We would never run out. I would make sure.

AT WORK I NEVER GOT to see the transformations of individual people. I don't know that transformations ever happened. Sometimes it seemed like the amount of food we gave out was just enough to keep people hungry, just enough to keep families coming back every month. It wasn't the goal to make lifelong customers out of food bank clients—our CEO used to say that the goal was to put ourselves out of business—but the food lines never got shorter.

My job was mostly to raise money, to persuade the people who still had jobs during the pandemic to donate their extra jars of peanut butter and pasta sauce. Often, I wished I could tell the full truth: that sometimes it wasn't enough. That a man had every right to be mad when he reached the front of the line and there was no food left except a single bag of salad. Maybe it wasn't fair for him to be mad at us, at the volunteers, at the government funding, at the community donors, at whoever donated a bag of salad. But he was mad for a reason: mad at whatever circumstances kept him in a world where he had to wait three hours in a line of traffic, where a pandemic was making him poorer than usual, where he couldn't afford the most basic of resources to keep himself alive. Of course he was mad.

Increasingly people were stealing. Someone broke into my car at work and took the jacket I had stashed in the back seat. Who could blame them? At the corner store near work I would see people stealing water bottles and dog food and cans of beans. Sometimes the police showed up. Sometimes older women would cluster in the candy aisle, shaking their heads at what the world had come to. *When did people get so rude?* they would say. *Why do people have to steal?*

Eventually I learned that my therapist had worked as a dog groomer at some point—all her talk of resource guarding, everything she knew about animal behavior. For a while it had offended me, how often she compared me to a dog. *Every behavior serves a purpose*, she would say. She meant that an animal is never acting out just for fun, never being bad just for the sake of it. *Animals don't know bad*, she'd say.

She meant that all the things that look like aggression or meanness are just messages communicating fear or anxiety or hunger or pain. I would tell her about Monkey, how she had started to relax around the other cats, and my therapist would stare at me through the screen in the way that meant she wanted me to figure something out for myself without her having to say it.

Do you think . . . ? she would prompt me, and I would stare dumbly back at her, thinking only about Monkey and hunger and the price of cat food. *Do you think that if you had the security of knowing you would always be fed, and you would always have shelter, and you didn't have to worry about these basic parts of survival . . . ?*

I finished for her: *I would be different.*

MONKEY TURNED OUT TO BE a weird, goofy little cat. After months of regular meals, she started climbing trees and smirking down at me from the tallest branches. She started waiting outside my door for attention, waiting to see which toy I would bring her. Her favorite thing was rolling in the dirt, and she would do it over and over again, even when it was dinnertime, even when the other cats were eating. I would put down bowls of food and Monkey would be unbothered by it, on her back in the dirt, her white belly in the air, bending her body nearly in half to wiggle back and forth on the ground.

You're a goof now, I would tell her, and she would flip upright, her eyes manic and flashing, and sprint away. She had a bizarre way of running, like the back half of her body couldn't keep up with the front. She'd bomb around the yard gracelessly, crashing into things, having fun. There was no part left of her that was a bully. No part of her that was mean.

One day I admitted on Instagram that Monkey had once been my least favorite of the cats—she was mean, a bully, always smacking me—and no one who had known her since could understand. *She's such a sweet cat*, people would say. *She's just a little goof!*

And it was true. Everything I knew about Monkey when she was starving had nothing to do with what she actually was. Everything I thought was her personality was just the way she was trying to survive.

AT WORK I HAD STARTED to imagine what each person would be doing with their time if they didn't have to wait three hours for food. All those kids in the back seat—would they be playing? Learning? Sleeping? Did their developing brains understand what they were in line for? Would it shape them, their future responses to food, their capacity for kindness and creativity? How much space in their brain was occupied by hunger, by the reminder that there wasn't enough, by the sad fact of the single packet of instant oatmeal?

The people who flipped us off, the people who said *Fuck you*. The people who were rude and arguing, stealing from the corner store, running from the cops. I wondered what they would be like if they had everything they needed. The promise of it: that they would never be without.

Sometimes at work I tried to tell people about Monkey, but it mostly seemed to make me sound insane. *This cat is nice now!* I was always saying, like it meant something. I was practicing my own niceness, trying to keep my cabinets stocked, inventorying the snacks I kept stashed in my desk. Trying to keep the cats fed. Trying to share cookies when I could. Wondering what I could be like.

Men Call Cats Sluts

Before I moved to Poets Square, I had never seen a female cat in heat. Some of the cats outside our house would get a little more affectionate with the male cats, roll over in the dirt for attention, stretch their front paws out luxuriously, raising their rears, shaking their tails. Some of them would howl into the night for a mate. They were insistent, ambushing the male cats, walking in front of them again and again, throwing themselves down in the dirt, shaking and yowling and insisting. Begging for it.

Oh yeah, a friend said, when I realized the cats were all going into heat. *Cats get super slutty about it.*

I had been watching Mini, a skinny gray and white cat with enormous yellow eyes. She seemed to always be in heat and I didn't understand it, the cats' cycles, anything about how they reproduced. Mini seemed to be disoriented by her own actions: she was shaking her butt, holding her tail up, chirping at the male cats who had gathered to watch her. She kept looking over at me, bewildered. She couldn't stop. She wouldn't stop until she was pregnant.

I LEARNED LATER THAT the first thing you should do when you find stray cats—before you give them silly names, before you spend all your extra money on cat toys, definitely before you make an Instagram account for them—is get them fixed. I had done everything wrong. I knew, theoretically, about the importance of spaying and neutering animals, but I had no understanding of the urgency of it, how rapidly and repeatedly the cats would reproduce. How much their behavior would change.

Mini was the first cat I trapped at our house. She didn't even have a name then; I was calling her Gray and White Cat #3. She always had a frantic look in her eyes, a hypervigilance she developed to survive on the streets. She was scared of most things, jumpy around the other cats, but she seemed to figure out pretty quickly that I was safe. That my presence meant food. I would stay very still around her, moving slowly to put food in front of her, and she would gulp it down, staring up at me with her giant yellow eyes.

After she was spayed, the change in Mini was immediate. She had been prowling the yard with her tail in the air, quivering, calling for the male cats. She had been pregnant and then pregnant again and then pregnant again, hounded by the other cats, mounted by the males each time she was back in heat. How she yowled, all those nights, drawing every cat in the neighborhood toward her, looking scared as they approached. And then she didn't. After she was spayed, she slept unbothered in the driveway. She rested. She rolled, sometimes, in the warm dirt outside our front door, her gray fur looking dull from the dust, and she closed her eyes, as if for the first time in her life she didn't have to keep watch.

It was a thing I hadn't known existed, that constant awareness in animals, how the cats were always following their instincts and confused by them at the same time, exhausted by them, creating more and more kittens in our driveway and then watching them struggle to survive, like they hadn't meant to do that at all. And the way it could be quieted so quickly with a trip to the vet.

Mini was first. Lola was next: the humane trap, the drive to the vet. Then François and Hambone, both male cats, who a few weeks after their neuters stopped fighting each other, stopped chasing the female cats around.

It took me months to get through all thirty cats at the house, months to quiet all the urges, working as quickly as I could to get them all to the vet faster than they could reproduce. Each cat, when they were under anesthesia to be sterilized, got a little notch in their left ear: the universal sign that an outdoor cat had been spayed or neutered. I was proud of those ear tips, proud of what they signaled to anyone walking by our house. *I am taking care of these cats*, the ear tips said. *I am doing something about this.* In the driveway, Mini had started sleeping with her belly in the air. In the driveway there were no new kittens.

I HAD NO INTENTION of becoming a volunteer cat trapper; I didn't even know that was a thing anyone could be. I hadn't really even meant to get so involved with the cats outside our house; I still looked around at the cases of cat food piled in our kitchen, at the piles of cat poop I raked up from the yard every day, and found myself thinking: *How did I end up here?*

I was outside our house one night feeding the cats, watching them all scramble from their beds to their bowls. A neighbor was walking by and stopped at the edge of the driveway. He lived a few houses south of us, he told me, and had seen me outside with the cats. His name was Ray. He asked: *Are you the cat lady?*

I made a face. I wasn't sure.

He said: *I have cats in my yard, too. Can you help?*

Ray had eight cats living in his yard and his garage. He had started with two but then both of them gave birth. One of them lived inside the ceiling of his garage and was pregnant again already. He called her Little Girl.

I don't even know how she keeps getting pregnant, Ray said. *She never leaves the space inside the ceiling.*

For a week I spent every evening walking down the street to Ray's house, my traps tucked under my arms. We set the traps together and waited, listening for the sounds of Little Girl descending from the ceiling, for the distinct metal clink of the trap closing behind her. Ray couldn't stop talking about the cats, how tenderly he cared for them, how they were almost like his family. As we waited, he showed me his old prison tattoos, talked about the drugs he used to use, how proud he was now of his grandkids.

When we finally heard it—the rustling thumps in the ceiling beams, the clink of the trap—Ray was emotional. *My girl*, he said, peering in at her inside the trap. Little Girl was fluffy and brown, big wisps of fur unfurling around her neck, and in the trap she looked surly, like she couldn't believe she had been tricked. The rest of the cats were her babies and her grandbabies and her great-grandbabies.

She had been doing it for years: going into heat, descending from the ceiling until she was pregnant again. Raising crawl-space babies.

What a strange intimacy it was, all the nights I spent outside Ray's garage in the dark. He was sweet. I was glad to have met a neighbor, glad to know someone else who was kind to the cats in our neighborhood. That last night at his house I turned to walk home in the dark.

You know, Ray said as I turned, nodding like he had something serious to say before I left. *With your figure you could have been a titty dancer.*

———

I STARTED RESPONDING TO OTHER NEIGHBORS who needed help: people in my neighborhood, people who messaged me on Instagram or posted on Nextdoor about the kittens they had found under their shed.

By then it was springtime: kitten season. The thousands of stray cats across the city were all going into heat at the same time and kittens were pouring out of them, overwhelming shelters, dying in the streets.

I started showing up at strangers' houses with two traps in the back of my car. It was almost always women who asked for help with cats, and almost always men—their boyfriends and husbands and teenage sons—who lurked weirdly in the background, acting like it was an inconvenience to have me there, like I had somehow caused them to have stray cats show up in their yard. Like I might be both insane and contagious. *Ah*, the husbands would say, opening the door when I knocked. *You're the cat lady?*

It was true that I was a woman and I was caring for thirty cats, and by that point I was usually driving around with a few cat traps in my car, a few cans of tuna tucked in the glove compartment. I understood I fit the description. But from the beginning I bristled at the term.

Do you get paid for this? people were always asking. *Is this your job?*

It wasn't, but I found it more fulfilling than the work I was doing at the food bank, writing content to raise money. At work I mostly stared at a screen and tried to feel like what I was doing made a difference, that it added up into something good. With the cats I could quantify my impact: three cats spayed and neutered, ten cats spayed and neutered, twenty cats spayed and neutered. At home I could see the difference it made: all night we used to hear the yowling, the fighting and mating, the horrible chirps and howls and hisses. Now it was quiet. The female cats, toward whom I couldn't help but feel extra sympathetic, seemed like they were resting for the first time in their lives.

EVERYONE WAS ALWAYS ASKING what Tim thought of the cats. It was always the first question, before they asked why we had so many cats or how I had gotten involved in helping them or what it was like to spend several nights a week in other people's yards, catching cats. I could tell someone that I was caring for thirty feral cats, or that last month I had helped spay and neuter over a hundred cats, or that I had just saved nine kittens who would have otherwise been crushed to death, and before being impressed or curious or sad they would raise their eyebrows and say: *Hmm. What does Tim think?*

Even people who followed me on Instagram, people I didn't

even know. Strangers were always asking me: *What does your boyfriend think of the cats?*

I hated the implication—that men didn't like cats, or would begrudge their partner the tenderness it took to sit all night in the driveway, petting the tiny heads of the kittens that kept being born. Or that it mattered, that the most important factor in trying to save the lives of abandoned animals was my boyfriend's approval. That I would stop if he asked.

More than that I hated that the implication was close to being right. Tim didn't hate cats—he spent plenty of time with me in the driveway, waving feathered cat toys and petting the kittens, his hands looking enormous against them—but he was dubious about either of us taking on the responsibility of caring for them. It was a large thing to add to our lives. We had been dating for less than a year and newly moved in together.

We set a boundary right away: no cats inside the house. We already had Maggie, my old rescue dog, and she enforced the boundary, snarling at the door when the cats got too close. Over time I stretched the boundary in emergencies: an injured cat resting in the bathroom overnight until his vet appointment in the morning, a few bottle-fed kittens in a crate in the laundry room. Just for a few nights. *What does Tim think about that?* everyone would ask, eyebrows raised.

As I started trapping more cats, waiting in line at more spay and neuter clinics, meeting other rescuers and fosters and people who had inherited large numbers of feral cats, the pattern kept repeating. All the cat people I met were women. All the women were thinking about adopting another cat, fostering another litter of kittens, volunteering more hours to help more animals. And all of them had the same reason not to: their male partners. *I wish!* they were always saying, when they had to say no to a cat who needed help. *My husband would kill me.*

Tim's hobby was mountain biking and the number of bikes he had took up a whole room in our house. Then the bike chains and helmets and tire pumps gradually took over our house, his spandex jerseys always hung over our kitchen chairs to dry, tread marks appearing on our walls where he wheeled the muddy tires through the house. He left for long weekend races up north and was up at four thirty every Saturday morning for six-hour rides. Everyone was always impressed by his commitment to riding. No one ever asked what I thought.

―――

THE MORE NIGHTS I SPENT trapping feral cats all over the city, the more I got hit on, often by men I probably wouldn't have otherwise met. *Expanding your horizons*, a friend told me.

I had been trapping with Brad for over a month, working our way through the dozens of cats that had been reproducing for years in the junkyard behind his house. He was finally cleaning it up, finally sorting scrap metal and crushing the rusting frames of old cars, and he kept finding kittens. Litter after litter, their moms all mixing together so we didn't know who belonged to who. Brad had been working alongside me, learning how the traps worked, texting me updates. I was making daily trips to his property, dropping off the cats that had just been fixed and then catching a few more for the next round. He had started leaving his back gate open for me, so I didn't have to wait for him. *I'm trusting you*, he told me, with a friendly wink. *I wouldn't let just anyone back here.*

Brad's texts started straying into other topics: an offhand comment about the weather, his hopes that I was having a lovely day. He was in his sixties, I guessed, and good-natured. He lived alone—just Brad and his junkyard and his forty-eight cats. It wasn't my job to make any assumptions about his life.

There were eight cats left to spay and neuter. I saw a text from Brad and I opened it without thinking, expecting an update on the newest litter of kittens we were monitoring.

Listen, the text read. *I rented a hotel room for the day. If you're interested.*

I stared at the text, waiting for the follow-up message that would tell me he had sent it to the wrong person. Two of his cats were still at the vet. I was supposed to bring them back to him that night.

My phone lit up again. It was Brad. The text said: *I can keep a secret ;)*

———

THE CASUAL MISOGYNY OF CAT RESCUE wasn't new to me. It was the same misogyny I had experienced when I worked at the front desk of a mostly male gym, the same sexism as the office politics at my desk job, just another variation of the low-level fear I kept with me anywhere I walked alone. There was nothing shocking about it.

What I didn't expect was the way the misogyny was directed at the cats themselves. I was used to hearing human women slut-shamed; it was new to me that men would call cats sluts.

I would arrive to help catch a pregnant stray and the discussion happening around me was about how often that same cat got pregnant again and again, how frequently she was in heat, displaying herself to the male cats. *She's constantly knocked up*, they would say. *She can't keep it in her pants!*

Men would watch cats in heat, cats holding their butts in the air and shaking their tails, while I set my cat traps with tuna, arranged them to entice the cats so I could get them spayed. *She's shaking it like a stripper*, the men would say. *This one's a little whore.*

When the men were husbands or boyfriends, their female partners would give them a playful slap. *She's a cat*, the women would say. *Don't be gross.*

There was something sickening about how easily the word slipped from men's mouths, how casually they could call a cat a whore. It wouldn't have occurred to me, ever, to apply the word to an animal. *Who else are you calling sluts?* I always wanted to ask, knowing that I didn't want to know the answer. *How often?*

———

MINI STARTED TRYING TO MEOW at me, although no sound ever came out of her. She didn't trust me, not entirely, but when I opened the door with breakfast she would open her mouth at me. I could tell she was young by how perfect her teeth were, how white against the pink of her mouth when she meowed. I was always amazed at how quiet she was, how silently she could sneak around the yard. *Mini girl*, I would say to her, and she would open her mouth in response.

Once, I got a call about a cat who was actively in labor, struggling, her tiny wet kitten half out of her. I got there as fast as I could and saw a group of men wearing tracksuits, standing around in a courtyard lifting weights on improvised benches, towels thrown over their shoulders. I approached them because I had to. I asked if they knew about the cat, if they knew where she was. *That's our cat*, they said, and they told me to leave.

If she needs medical care I can help, I told them. *I'll bring her back.*

I explained about spaying, about making sure she didn't have to keep having kittens, again and again, in their barren, dusty courtyard.

No, no, they said. *That's just what she does. She's always having kittens.*

She's a slutty little girl, one of the men said, and they all laughed.

One of the men, taking off his track jacket to show just an undershirt underneath, took a step toward me. *She's a slutty little girl,* he repeated, and then he nodded toward me. *And what about you?*

———

WHEN I STARTED TRAPPING CATS, I had been wearing a fake wedding band for years to discourage male attention. It mostly hadn't made a difference in coffee shops or bars, when men either didn't notice it or didn't care. But once I was working with cats every man seemed to key in on it right away, to question it. Sometimes I was catching cats in alleys behind businesses late at night. *Your husband lets you be out here alone?* men would say. Or, if I was in their yard, setting my traps on their little patios, around their grills and piles of firewood, they would be bolder. It was clear their questions had nothing to do with my safety. *Married, huh?* they would say. *What does your husband think of having so many cats?*

Does your husband know you're with another man right now? men would say, and they'd wink, or laugh, or stay straight-faced, waiting for my reaction. In order to help the cats I mostly had to put up with it. The little female cats in heat, desperate and pacing at the edges of alleys, still nursing their last litter and already pregnant with the next, the huge male tomcats stalking them every night, never letting them rest. I would catch the eye of those cats and I would use all my energy to communicate with them, to try to send them a telepathic message: *Go get in that trap, sweet girl. I will get you spayed. It will be better than this.*

CATS ARE SO WIDELY UNDERSTOOD as a sign that a woman is single. It's such a common trope in TV shows and movies: a woman gives up on love, accepts a lifetime of loneliness, adopts a couple of cats. If you use the tax software TurboTax, one of the first questions it will ask is about your filing status: single, married, divorced, legally separated. Each choice has a little cartoon graphic with it: *married* is a pair of wedding rings; *divorced* is a scroll of paper, like a certificate; *legally separated* is a roadway diverging into two paths. *Single* is a person, standing alone, with a cat.

Sometimes people seem amazed that I'm not single, as if worrying about the stray cats outside my house is fundamentally incompatible with a romantic relationship. Sometimes people seem shocked that anyone cares about stray cats at all, like the cats yowling on the streets could be a talisman against finding love. Like they could put out a bowl of cat food and instantly be doomed.

And *single*, as it's signaled by cats, is also supposed to imply *sexless*. Which means that men—even in joking, unserious ways—will simultaneously slut-shame a stray cat for the biology that forces her to seek out a mate, and stereotype as sexless any woman who scoops up that stray cat for a trip to the vet. Too much sex, not enough sex.

I encountered all sorts of weird confusions about human sexuality and cat biology, and it was absurd to have to sort them out: the men who didn't want to neuter cats because then they couldn't "enjoy life with the females," the women who thought it was funny to watch a female cat scream as she was mounted by a male. All of it was tangled up for me with the way men spoke to me about cats, or to cats about me. *Come here, Fluffy*, men would say when I was there to scoop up the newest litter of stray kittens born under their deck. *This beautiful young lady is here to help you.*

Women sometimes seemed embarrassed to see cats in heat, twisting their hands and turning red when they described to me what the cats in their backyards were doing. *I don't know what to do about the black cat*, a woman would say to me. *We raised her first litter of kittens, but she keeps doing it again, she's out there every night, she won't stop.* Her husband snickering in the background.

The other women who trapped cats with me seemed embarrassed sometimes too, like they had gotten suckered into helping cats but understood they now fit a stereotype. For some women it was a point of pride; they wore T-shirts that said *Crazy Cat Lady* and made jokes about kicking their husbands out to make room for more cats.

The male cats who had never been neutered would show up looking like old teddy bears, their cheeks inflated over time from testosterone, their necks and faces scarred from years of fighting. Their floppy cauliflower ears. *He's such a boy*, women would say, when a feral tom was puffed up and angry in a dark alley, defending his space, on guard. *So aggressive.* I was always explaining to people that those male cats spent all their time fighting and fathering kittens, that their lives could be so much softer once they were neutered. *No*, men would say, as offended as if I had suggested neutering all human men. *He spends all his time mating? Good for him.*

AT OUR HOUSE ALL THE CATS were calm. Mini had been a lean cat, long and slinky like a ferret, and a few months after she was spayed, she finally started putting on weight. Most nights Tim went to bed by eight so he could wake early for a bike ride, and instead of getting in bed with him I would creep out to the carport and stretch my hand toward Mini, move her food bowl closer and closer to me, until one night I reached out and instead of running she sniffed my hand. She let me touch her, flinching just a little as I ran my hand over her back. She was softer than I expected, her eyes less frantic, and instead of running from my touch she relaxed—I could feel it, the way her whole body was tense and then wasn't—and I watched as her giant yellow eyes closed once, and then again. She looked up at me, slow-blinking her trust, and lay down right in front of me. I spent hours with her this way, so many nights, my chest swelling with tenderness and pride and contentment, how much she had changed, how I had helped her, how we were both vulnerable little creatures who just wanted to feel safe.

I tried to explain it to people I knew, how meaningful it was to see so much change in such a small cat. How much gentleness she deserved. *Wait*, people said. *You don't go to bed when Tim does? You don't get in bed together?* They would narrow their eyes like I had admitted to witchcraft. *Does that bother him?*

―――――

FOR A MONTH, A MAN named Scott had been sending me pictures of his cat's nipples. She had just given birth and they were engorged, the way they should be on any nursing mammal. *Look at her nips today*, he would text me, with a picture zoomed in on her double rows of teats.

They look fine, I would respond, unsure what he was getting at. *Keep the kittens with her until they're a little older.*

I know, he'd text back. *Just funny to look at. She's got her boobies hanging out. Needs to cover up!*

I was careful to stay covered up. Tim was always reminding me to carry pepper spray, but I didn't know how to explain that the threat wasn't physical violence. Most of the time it wasn't even actual advances. The men I worked with were often friendly, sometimes kind; they called cats sluts so casually that it was clear they didn't intend to mean anything by it. Like they were making a joke.

My daily exhaustion was more about the kind of humoring I had to do just to get my job done, the things I nodded along to in service of keeping myself safe. Sometimes I wondered if my inclination to help stray cats came from my own desire for security, how vulnerable I felt in the world, how I longed for someone to scoop me up and keep me safe. The way Mini had always been on high alert, her hypervigilance to every movement around her.

With men I would wordlessly agree: sure, the cat I was trying to catch was a whore. Sure, a female cat has body parts comparable to mine. Surely, I was reminded every day, it was my job to entertain men long enough to spay the stray cats that were living in their yards. The threat was the reminder that I was not in control. The threat was the reminder that to so many men I was exactly as powerless as a stray cat wailing on the streets.

Sad Boy and Lola

Sad Boy appeared each night like the moon, rising large and white over our roof. He was a feral cat but he looked like an ancient god, enormous and weathered, his scarred cheeks, his sleepy eyes. He was the oldest and largest cat I had ever seen, wild and shy, perched on the edge of our roof with his massive paws dangling down in front of him. He was always watching.

Sad Boy was never alone. He was followed—maybe guarded—at all times by Lola, a giant brown tabby. She was Sad Boy's bodyguard and lover, companion and protector and mate. She was a darker cat, her tail turning to black at the tip, and she blended in with the night, so some days after dark I would look up at the roof and see only Sad Boy—my moon god, my giant wise man—until I squinted and waited, letting my eyes adjust to the dark. And then I could see her: Lola, her glowing eyes, the outline of her body next to his. They were always on the roof together. It always looked like they were watching the stars.

It was rare to see them apart, Sad Boy and Lola. In the early morning, they would descend from their rooftop like royalty—first Sad Boy, and then Lola close behind him, following his exact footsteps, placing her paws where his had been—and eat the breakfast I left out for them, and then they would sit together and lick their paws in perfect unison, each of them raising their left paw and then their right. Sad Boy would fall asleep, his ancient white body like a pile of melting ice cream, and Lola would tend to him, cleaning his ears, licking the spot between his eyes. I'm not exaggerating when I say that they would hold hands: stretched out on their shared bed on our patio, spooning each other, her giant brown paw on top of his giant white one.

Watching Sad Boy and Lola together was almost unnerving in its sweetness, how gentle they were with each other, how they were never apart.

Who could have guessed, someone commented online, *that true love was invented by a pair of feral cats in Arizona?*

HERE'S AN EARLY LESSON I LEARNED about love.

When I was twenty-one I was working at a local gym for the summer, wiping down treadmills eight hours a day. One of the gym regulars—blond hair, wide smile—was sitting at the chest press. I was looking at his forearms. When I walked by wearing colorful sneakers, he caught my eye and nodded at my shoes and said: *Sweet kicks.*

After that we chatted at the front desk every time he came in. His name was Robby. He didn't tell me at first how old he was, and I didn't mention that I had just finished college. On our first date he took me to our small-town airport, where he had access to all the runways because he sometimes flew a friend's single-engine plane. We had stopped for ice cream on the way there, little sundaes in take-out containers with plastic spoons. As it got dark, we sat on the runway, right in the middle of it, and he flipped a switch and the runway lights lit up on either side of us, stretching out in dotted lines into the dark.

It was thrilling.

We stayed there for hours, talking about things that felt deep and important and mature, the kind of first date that only happened in movies. We were sitting cross-legged on the tarmac, facing each other, holding hands. He swore he saw a shooting star over my shoulder. Sometime after midnight we walked back to his car, and he looked very serious. *I never do this*, he told me, and we kissed.

BEFORE I REALIZED THAT THEY were always together, I separated Sad Boy and Lola. I didn't know better. They were two cats out of the thirty I had suddenly inherited and I hadn't yet parsed all the social dynamics between them. I only knew then that Lola was pregnant and had walked into a trap, and after a trip to the vet to get spayed, a local rescuer had offered her spare bedroom for Lola to recover indoors.

Lola was away for a month. Sad Boy appeared occasionally in the backyard, looking filthy and gray. I don't know how to describe him except as downtrodden and moping. He had stopped grooming himself. He was losing weight, sitting by himself on the roof at night, looking lost.

Lola stopped eating, too. She was stressed and shut down, her eyes getting duller by the day.

She's deteriorating, the rescuer told me. *She's giving up.*

We didn't know why. We didn't know what Lola was missing, what Sad Boy was waiting for.

We brought Lola back to our house and she was still inside the carrier, sitting outside the front door, when Sad Boy appeared at the end of the driveway. I had never seen him there before; he never showed up in our front yard, or this close to me, or in daylight. *What is he doing here?* I wondered, and I watched as he sat there, stoic, sniffing the air. Lola had crushed herself into the back corner of the carrier, trying to hide, but suddenly she approached the door. Sniffed.

They both perked up. I was looking back and forth between them, Sad Boy and Lola, watching their noses working, watching them realize the other was near. Lola was making a chirping noise I had never heard from her before. Sad Boy was swiveling his ears toward the sound. I knew I was witnessing something but I wasn't sure what.

I let Lola out of the carrier and she disappeared into the dark. The next morning, they were together on the roof: Sad Boy and Lola. Sad Boy was spectacularly white again, gleaming in the sun, licked clean. He looked fluffy, like he had been bathed and blow-dried. Lola had her paws tucked under her and her tail curled around Sad Boy's body. Something was happening between them—some bond, some contentedness—that seemed beyond my understanding.

I'm sorry, I told them, and they blinked down at me from the roof.

MY BIRTHDAY WAS A FEW WEEKS after that first date with Robby. I was turning twenty-two. He had mentioned his age casually, slipped it into conversation after we had already kissed, after the airport lights had already hypnotized me. He was thirty-five.

On my birthday I was working late at the gym, filling out new membership forms at the front desk, and Robby dropped by to leave a cupcake and a card. He didn't even say anything—just ducked inside, slid a cupcake across the front desk, winked at me—and left again. My coworkers waggled their eyebrows and made faces and I blushed.

It had seemed like a good sign. I only knew how to divide people into two categories—good or bad—and a person who brings you a cupcake on your birthday is *good*. It was that simple in my mind.

I was living with my parents that summer, collecting thrifted dishes and bookcases to move in to my grad school apartment in a month. I was starry-eyed about all of it, telling my mom about Robby: about the airport, the runway lights, how much we had in common. *Neither of us were looking for a relationship*, I told her, like I knew anything. *But these things happen.*

I was leaving out his age, trying to stay vague, but she caught me. *How old is he?* she asked, and before I even answered she understood my pause to mean there was a reason I didn't want to tell her. She said: *Why do you think a thirty-five-year-old man would be interested in a twenty-two-year-old girl?*

I was taken aback. I was insulted.

Because we connected with each other, I told her. And we had: that first night at the airport we had talked about our whole lives, everything that had ever happened to us, our entire histories and futures. *What are we doing*, we had asked each other, giggling, intertwining our fingers. It wasn't my problem if my mom didn't get it.

I was moving out in a month. I was starting a new semester, a new job, a new start at everything. I had Robby.

———

THE STORY OF SAD BOY and Lola was the first of my cat stories to get internet attention. It was hard not to become instantly enamored with Sad Boy—an ancient street cat who looked like he contained all the wisdom in the universe—and his feral wife who would die to protect him.

He has a wife?! people would say, and I would share videos of Lola protecting him, grooming him, dropping toys at his feet. Sad Boy never hunted or played—he was too old, too placid and serene—but Lola would run around the yard collecting crickets in her mouth and bring them back to him like offerings. She would stretch out in front of him, and Sad Boy would rest his chin on her like a pillow.

Lady and the Tramp if they were feral cats, people commented. *The greatest love story of our generation.*

I made sure everything I bought for them was big enough for two: an extra-large cat house, the biggest cat tower available, a dog-size bed. They took up residence on our back patio and every night I fed them from matching bowls, side by side, and watched through the window as they shared their dinner and licked each other clean.

Sad Boy was usually the first to fall asleep on their enormous patio bed, and every time Lola would walk across the bed to join him, she left a little trail of pawprints on the plush fabric. That was the view from my kitchen window every night around dinnertime, just before dusk: this big velvet bed, these two cats inexplicably in love, a little path of pawprints across their pillows.

WHEN I WASN'T WORKING AT the gym I was running there, logging long miles on the treadmill. Robby and I both adjusted our schedules so we could see as much of each other as possible, but I wouldn't give up my runs. *Of course*, he said, when I would tell him I had to get my run in before I went to his apartment for the night. *I love that you're passionate about running.* A good sign, I thought.

Later, he would ask me not to wear the spandex shorts I always wore.

I don't trust other guys around you, he would say. *I've seen how you look in those shorts.*

I was twenty-two, obsessed with running, obsessed with how my body looked to other people. I was flattered, somehow, or maybe I thought he was joking, or maybe it was so foreign to me, that he would tell me not to wear the thing I wore every single day, that it didn't even register. I wore the shorts the next day anyway, and when I finished my run and checked my phone, still standing on the treadmill, I had a text from Robby.

You wore the shorts.

I looked around.

I saw you.

I didn't understand.

Later, he would claim that he had stopped by the gym to say hi, to bring me a present, and then he saw me in those shorts and was so hurt, was so disappointed that I would do that to him, that he left before I saw him. It felt bad, all of it, but I had already categorized him in my head as *good* and I wasn't able to hold any nuance, to realize that he had done nice things and now was doing something bad.

He explained it away. I think I apologized. I was confused, but I had felt confused around other people all my life, in every friendship and every social situation, always feeling like I wasn't quite following the same script that everyone else had access to. Of course it had been my fault; I was the one who had misunderstood something. We had a good thing going, me and Robby, and I didn't want to be the one to ruin it.

I'm sorry, I told him, and I stopped wearing the shorts.

SAD BOY AND LOLA BOTH hated me, or maybe feared me. They were both feral; they had grown up outside with no human contact, and they mostly had no idea what to make of me. I couldn't get close to them. I had stopped using our patio completely; when we had first moved in I had loved it, the little shaded ramada and the flowering vines that grew over it, and I had bought lawn chairs and little tables. I had imagined myself reading there on spring afternoons, maybe adding a hammock.

Instead, I filled the space with cat towers and beds, water bowls and toys. If I stepped outside into the yard—even turned the doorknob of the back door—both Sad Boy and Lola would flee, escape to their roof, where they knew I couldn't reach them. I mostly stayed inside and let them take over the patio. I bought a cat-size hammock and they slept in it, both of them, swaying just a little in the breeze.

In the winter I added a heating pad to the giant cat bed on the patio. It was on a timer that would turn on every night as the sun went down, but I didn't trust the timer. Too many nights I lay in bed, cozy against the weather, wondering if that was the night the timer would fail and the heating pad wouldn't turn on and Sad Boy and Lola would be curled on a cold bed, not understanding why it never warmed up. Too many nights I would get out of bed in the dark, sneak to the backyard barefoot, freezing my feet just long enough to double-check the heating pad. In the dark, curled together, entirely incapable of interpreting my presence as anything like love, Sad Boy and Lola would hiss at me.

Online, people kept asking: *Why would you have cats that don't love you back?*

I didn't know how to explain the late nights, the lying awake, the watching worriedly from windows to make sure they were both getting enough to eat. The wild emotion of watching them walk through the garden together, tails intertwined. Sometimes watching them felt significant, these two feral cats, like I was witnessing something I wasn't supposed to see. Watching them love each other, washing my hands where they scratched me.

I never learned what to expect from love. What are we supposed to tolerate? What do we deserve in return?

———

THE DAY I MOVED INTO my new apartment Robby wasn't speaking to me. I don't remember why except that we had been driving somewhere for dinner and something I said had upset him.

We had been together for a month and had spent every day of it together, twelve hours at a time, dinner dates that stretched into mornings. He flew me a few states over just to get ice cream, took me skydiving, paid for everything. When I admired a piece of art in his apartment, he took it off the wall and handed it to me. *It's yours*, he told me, and I was enamored.

That night that we fought, I didn't know what had happened, what I had said wrong. As he got angrier I was frantic and confused, trying to trace the conversation back to where it had fallen apart, watching the last month of perfect dates, this perfect man, fall apart. *Wait*, I said, trying to catch up, and somehow it made him angrier, and he drove faster in the dark, reckless, weaving between cars.

Can we pull over? I asked him. *Can you slow down?*

He stared straight ahead. He said: *Which one of us is in the driver's seat?*

Something had shifted in a way I couldn't understand.

You, I said, and my voice sounded small.

My parents helped me move my new desk, my new bookcases. My mom was fussy, testing the burners on the stove, opening every cabinet. It was my first time living on my own and I had felt okay about it because of Robby; dating him had felt adult and now instead I was a kid in time-out, confused, unsure when my punishment would be over. Robby had said: *You know, maybe I need to think about this* and he had dropped me off at home without dinner and now it had been four days since I had heard from him.

My dad installed blinds in the new apartment, and I checked my phone again and again. And then my parents left, and it was just me and a pile of boxes in an empty apartment, and my phone was dark.

―――

ONCE, LOLA DISAPPEARED. I REALIZED she was missing because of Sad Boy's lonely wandering, like he was looking for her. That night I left their dinner on the patio and neither of them appeared. Neither of them ascended later to the roof; neither of them watched the stars. Instead, I found Sad Boy in the front yard, looking confused. He was such an old cat—fifteen, by a vet's estimate—and he had lived on the streets for every minute of it, and much of the time he looked dilapidated, run-down, like even he wasn't sure how he had made it that long.

Sad Boy was a slow-moving cat, and that night he ambled around the yard by himself, sniffing things. He didn't know where Lola was but he knew something was wrong. I stayed up late searching the yard, asking the neighbors if they had seen Lola. I was used to the roller coaster of grief and anxiety of loving feral cats: all the things that could go wrong, all the things about their environment I couldn't control. *She's fine*, I kept telling myself. *She'll be back*. But I couldn't explain the same thing to Sad Boy. He had climbed up to the roof by himself and was looking around in every direction, swiveling his head like an owl, like he was searching the neighborhood for her. There was no way to tell him that I was searching, too.

When I got up the next morning, Tim was on the roof. He was standing on the top rung of a ladder, perfectly still, a hand cupped to his ear. Lola's food from the night before was untouched. Sad Boy was still wandering alone. Tim looked solemnly down at me. He said: *I heard a meow*.

The sun wasn't up yet. The meow—so faint, a small pathetic cry—was coming from our neighbor's yard. We followed it, shaking treats, opening cans of cat food, begging Lola to make another noise so we could find her. It was me who found her: her big tabby body stuck between two wooden pallets, uninjured but unable to free herself. I lifted the top pallet, making enough room for her to get out, and I wanted so desperately for her to understand that I was helping her, that I would do anything for her, that I loved her. She was terrified.

Lola squirmed her way out as I held up the pallet, and she ran back to Sad Boy, and for years since I have been trying to hold on to the feeling of seeing them together that night on the roof, the pure relief, the way they were nuzzling each other so strongly, like they couldn't believe what had almost happened.

THE RELIEF WHEN ROBBY FINALLY called me again: it was like I had passed a test and was once again worth loving.

Sometime in my twenties I googled *how to know you're in love* and then read the results, feeling embarrassed. Feeling like you will die if a person doesn't text you back: is that love? Spiraling, pleading, unsure: is that love? Isn't it extravagant dates, ice cream sundaes and staying out until dawn, staying on the phone as we fell asleep? It was all-consuming, the way Robby had entered my life, and within a week I didn't know how to be without him. What had life been before Robby? How had I spent my days?

BOTH SAD BOY AND LOLA disliked other cats, which made their bond with each other more incredible. Lola would let out a high-pitched scream if another cat got within ten feet of her; she would hiss indiscriminately. Sad Boy would let the other cats get near but then shift uncomfortably, rocking on his paws, looking for Lola. There were thirty cats then, but it was never all thirty together; it was more like twenty-eight cats plus Sad Boy and Lola, separate, on the roof with only each other.

Cats are social animals, and bonded pairs like Sad Boy and Lola aren't uncommon. At first I would see them together and think how sweet, that some of the cats had friends. That some of them would split up into little cliques, that they had partners. But years later I still have not met another pair as bonded as Sad Boy and Lola, as incapable of functioning without each other, as sweetly melted together in a sleepy pile every morning on my patio.

For a long time my only goal was to get close enough to Sad Boy to get a good picture of him—his face, enormous and leonine, his body the color of a marshmallow—but every time I raised the camera Lola would appear out of nowhere and put her full body in front of his, keeping me away. Every evening they'd retreat again to the roof, sitting together like sphinxes, their eyes tracking the movement of moths as darkness fell. It never occurred to me before to wonder what stars looked like to wild animals. If sunsets are beautiful to cats.

———

ROBBY LIKED TO ASK QUESTIONS about my past, about who I had dated before him. It didn't matter what my answers were; they were automatically wrong. I would try to anticipate what he wanted to hear—*I didn't love them*, I would tell him. *They weren't as good as you. I've never had a boyfriend before, not like this, not like you*—and it didn't matter; the answer he wanted to hear was always whatever I didn't say. I would backpedal, change my answer, feeling the tension rising in the room with each word, walking back my story until it matched the one he wanted to hear, rewriting my own life until I was a blank page for him, and slowly the tension would defuse a bit, just enough for my panic to sink back down into my throat, and we would be back to normal. Back to eggshells.

It could be anything that set him off—we could be having a nice dinner and I could say the garlic bread was good and somehow this would start it all again. *Please*, I would say to him, and it took me ten years after our breakup to realize it was the begging he wanted. My crying, my misery, my utter dependence on him, the way I would fold instantly in any argument, anything to keep the peace. It was what he wanted.

I would say anything to keep Robby happy. I would say anything, but the subtext was always the same: *don't leave me, please don't leave me, please don't leave me alone.*

SOMETIME AFTER I FIRST SHARED the story of Sad Boy and Lola online, a stranger sent me a screenshot of her Tinder profile:

Lauren, 22
Looking for the Sad Boy to my Lola

On Halloween, a few people dressed as Sad Boy and Lola as a couple's costume: one white cat, one brown cat, always together. One girl sent me a picture of her and her boyfriend, their fabric tails intertwined. *We had to stay together all night,* she wrote, *because our tails were sewn together.*

I got an email from a name I didn't recognize with the subject line *wedding vows.*

My new husband and I both talked about Sad Boy and Lola in our vows this weekend, the email said. *I thought you would like to know that their love has been so inspiring to us.* There were photos attached, and when I clicked on one the file was so large that I was looking at a close-up of the bride's face stretched across my entire screen. I had to scroll to see her husband. They looked giddy and thrilled, laughing, like they were both trying to look at the camera but really only wanted to look at each other.

———

IT WAS A CAT THAT broke up me and Robby for real. It was our six-month anniversary, a Sunday at the end of the semester, and Robby wanted to see me.

I just can't do it, I told him. We were living an hour apart and driving back and forth to see each other. It was mostly me driving back and forth, because he didn't like my apartment. I was always rearranging, always buying furniture I couldn't afford to make my place look more adult for him.

Maybe later this week, I told Robby. He was upset about it, short on the other end of the phone in a way that a few months earlier would have sent me groveling, speeding straight to the highway to see him. But I was getting tired.

Instead, I spent that Sunday meeting an adoptable cat named Bubbles.

That night, Robby wouldn't answer my calls. He sent a string of angry texts.

You tell me you're too tired to see me and then you go out and you see a cat? he said, and there was something about the way he phrased it, like I had committed a mortal sin by looking at a cat.

I don't know what to tell you, I said, and I meant it. I had nothing left to give. It was a white flag.

I broke up with Robby and I adopted Bubbles.

Some time after that, in the first weeks of having a little creature sharing my apartment with me, sleeping curled against my body,

Robby texted me again. It almost worked. I almost saw him again, almost got dinner one more time at our favorite place, almost fell back into it.

I don't want to see that cat though, he said, and he told me how the cat had almost ruined us, how the cat would always remind him of the time I had screwed up, the time I had chosen to miss our anniversary. For months now Robby had been acting like I was the actual devil, something evil, like I was a cursed being that he alone could tolerate. I believed him. Who else could love me? What else could love mean?

But when he started to talk the same way about Bubbles, about my scruffy stray cat who was afraid of everything, it suddenly seemed ridiculous. Robby would curse Bubbles over the phone and I would stare incredulously at the cat, wondering how anyone could hold a grudge against a half-feral fluffy animal, his whiskers quivering when he purred. *He's just a little guy*, I would think. I suddenly saw how Robby had been treating me, how absurd it was to have believed I was a tiny thing beneath his thumb. That he had ever held any power over me.

ONCE, I REACHED TOO CLOSE to Sad Boy to set a bowl of cat food in front of him and he reared back and swatted at me hard with his claws out.

Online, someone commented: *Imagine making dinner for your boyfriend and he slaps the shit out of you. That would be abuse.*

Well, I responded, feeling annoyed. *A feral cat is not the same as a human man. Hope that helps.*

For a long time I thought about that word: *abuse*. I watched Sad

Boy and Lola from my window, the way he would paw gently at her for attention and she would turn to him, and they would touch their noses sweetly together. How tender they were with each other.

After we broke up, it took me years to realize how poorly Robby had treated me. It took me years after that to learn anything from it.

In the short term, in the months and years of my post-Robby early twenties, the lesson I learned was that if a relationship failed, it was my fault. If a relationship failed it was because I had said something wrong, had misinterpreted someone's tone, had failed to perform some task perfectly, the way a girlfriend should. I learned that relationships were darkly complex, that my role in them was to anticipate a man's anger and defuse it, that love was begging and unkind. That there was an undercurrent, always, of my unworthiness, my desperate scrambling to be good enough for it. To keep it this time. To deserve it.

FOR YEARS NOW I HAVE stared out my window every night in the dark, watching Sad Boy and Lola stroll together under the lights I strung up through the garden. I feel so stupid to say that I've learned anything about love from a pair of feral cats. Surely I should have learned sooner, and from people, from my own failed relationships. I should have learned about romantic love from my parents or from my friends' weddings or from the men who tried to love me. From the men who were mean to me and from the men I cheated on and from the men I claimed to love but didn't, not really.

I should have learned something about love from therapy, from all the sessions I spent dissecting myself, trying to figure out what I deserved and why I couldn't find it.

I know what two feral cats have isn't the same as a human romantic relationship. I know that Sad Boy and Lola don't ever have to argue about splitting bills or washing dishes. They don't have to support each other's careers or meet each other's families or discuss their shared values, where they want to be in five years. They want to be right there on my roof, still together, still licking each other's little heads.

———

THIS IS THE NEW STANDARD, BOYS, someone commented on a video of Sad Boy watching Lola eat. *You let your girl eat first. You protect her with your life.*

Someone commented: *Honestly this is setting the bar for me. I won't accept less than love like this.*

Someone commented: *If my relationship isn't like Sad Boy and Lola's, I don't want it.*

I hope I'm not the only one learning.

———

I WAS WITH TIM when we moved into the house, when we found all the cats, when we discovered Sad Boy and Lola. I'm still with him now. Sometimes I feel so incredibly stunted, with such a childlike understanding of what a relationship should be. Sometimes I feel shocked to realize that love is a thing you can learn together.

Sometimes it almost feels boring, the mundanity of a life together without the days of silence, the pleading, the arguments that would escalate into fear. The thrill of relief that would follow. I feel so even-keeled, sitting on a couch next to a man I'm not afraid of. I've begun to feel changed on a cellular level by the steady presence of love, like all the chaotic and bursting parts of me have been quieted.

I turned thirty-two with Tim, with Sad Boy, with Lola, and thought about how I still wasn't as old as the men who had dated me a decade earlier. About all the things I had misunderstood as love.

Once, we sat together on our own roof, the tallest part of it. Tim had dragged a ladder to the gutters to investigate a leak, and as the sun dipped he called down to me. *Babe*, he said. *Come up here with me.*

I thought he wanted to show me the leak, and I dragged myself miserably up the ladder. Tim was always trying to show me how things worked—how to change the oil in my car, how to check the water heater behind our bathroom—and I mostly didn't care but tried to humor him.

He would be animated as he explained things, pointing out parts of machines and why they worked the way they did, and I would feign interest, nodding like I understood. *Thanks for listening*, he would say after, with a little smile like he knew I had been thinking about something else the whole time, and it surprised me every time that he could tell. That he thanked me.

From the top of the ladder I could see Tim perched at the peak of our roof, smiling. *Come up*, he said, and I crawled to him on my hands and knees, nervous about how high we were. I sat next to him, waited for him to show me something. Sometimes I was still waiting for the other shoe to drop, wondering if he was mad at me, if everything was a trick. *What?* I asked him.

It's just a pretty view, he said. *I wanted you to see it.*

It didn't escape me, that we were next to each other on the roof. By then we had watched Sad Boy and Lola up there for years. Their sweetness together. The sunsets. We stayed on the roof until the sun was fully set, until we got cold in the dark, and then we descended, together, me placing my feet exactly where his had been on the ladder.

Sometimes it seems like the sweetness between the cats has seeped into me. Sometimes I feel like I deserve it.

Bubbles

It shouldn't have surprised me, that there were other people who cared about cats. It shouldn't have surprised me, either, how high the number of cats like mine was. All the half-friendly, semi-wild cats reproducing outside all over Tucson, needing all the same care as pet cats but with no one to provide it. After a year in Poets Square—a year of sitting alone in the dark of my driveway, just me and a million eyes around me—something happened: I learned that there were other people doing the same thing.

I had lived in Tucson for years and hadn't seen many stray cats until we moved to Poets Square, but after just a few months of caring for the cats at our house I understood how well they hid, how hard you had to look. I learned the clues they left: the cat-size holes in fences, the piles of dirt the cats scraped up when they peed, the single plastic bowl in a driveway. The glowing eyes at night.

Finding feral cat colonies became a skill of mine, and I quickly learned where to spot them: the dumpsters behind gas stations, the alleys between apartment buildings, the houses like mine. I could spot their people sometimes, too: the women slipping furtively behind a dumpster to leave a bowl of water, the volunteer trappers trying inconspicuously to watch the cats from their cars.

I had felt mostly alone in my quest to save the cats outside our house. There was no one prowling the backyard with me, peering over the neighbor's wall to watch for kittens. It was a niche hobby, standing around in the dark watching feral cats, figuring out how to catch them. Even my friends who loved cats mostly loved the ones who were nice to them, the sweet indoor pets; they were less interested in staring at my roof for an hour for a chance to glimpse a cat who would hiss and run away.

But the women behind dumpsters, the people watching from cars: there were so many of them. They had meetings. They had group chats. They had a map of all the stray cat spots all over the city; they had vans full of traps to help. It felt, meeting all the people who also sat in their driveways at night with cats, like I had been holding my breath for a year and I could finally release it. I didn't have to do this alone.

―――

A DECADE BEFORE I FOUND the cats in our driveway, before I met Tim, before I even moved to Tucson, I was living alone for the first time. It was the fall of 2012.

I was freshly out of college. It was my first time in my own apartment, my first time without my parents, my first year of graduate school for a degree I had pinned all my hopes on. The first time in my life living without any kind of pet, no constant soft presence I could count on. I was twenty-two.

I spent that fall semester alternately romanticizing my new life—my own apartment in a quaint New England college town, my classes in an old brick building—and falling apart, feeling overwhelmed and acutely alone. I was dating Robby but somehow felt more alone because of it; much of the time he was either making me feel worse about myself or not speaking to me at all.

I spent those months wishing I could adopt a cat. A cat felt like the answer to everything: I was lonely and overwhelmed and isolated, and every night I got a chill I couldn't shake, shivering even with a mountain of blankets on top of me. I thought everything would be better if I could have a warm creature curled next to me.

I longed so desperately for a cat that sometimes I would drive to PetSmart just to look at cat toys and cat beds and cat bowls. I couldn't afford any of it. Sometimes I would write down the prices, add in the cost of cat food and litter and vet bills, and then compare the notes to my monthly budget, which I mostly avoided looking at because my teaching stipend barely covered rent.

It was one of those PetSmart trips—a Friday night in January, after I had survived my first semester but wasn't sure I would survive the next—when I saw a flyer for an adoptable cat. *BUBBLES*, the ad said, above a grainy grayscale photo of a black cat. Bubbles had been found half feral, emerging from the woods a few towns over. Maureen, the woman who had saved him, was so desperate to find the right home for him that she was offering to pay for all of his food and vet bills. He weighed eighteen pounds. *Bubbles has only one flaw,* the ad said. *He likes to bite.*

I STARTED GRAD SCHOOL WITH an exact image in my head of how it would go. I had excelled in college, loved everything about reading and thinking and studying, but by my senior year I had started to feel like I was suffocating. I was still living with my parents, in my little Massachusetts hometown, spending time with friends who teased me for the nights I stayed home studying instead of socializing. I had begun to imagine grad school as a kind of utopia: challenging classes, a chance to teach, a group of peers who would love the same things I did. My mental image of the coming years was mostly about the people I would meet: the friends I would study with in the library, the writing groups we'd form around dining tables, the manuscripts we'd trade and the poetry readings we'd attend and the lifelong friends and colleagues who were right there, starting school that same year with me. It was all happening.

But when the semester started, I felt deeply underprepared for my classes. Everything I thought I knew was immediately dwarfed by everyone else's incredible intellect, and the apartment I had been so excited to make my own turned out to have a barely working toilet and a stove that smelled like burning hair. The biggest deviation from the image of my life I had constructed in my mind was the friends I would make, the community I would find. My classmates were exactly as I had imagined them: unbearably cool, hyperintelligent, fascinating in the things they knew and the conversations they could hold. And I felt like I didn't fit in with them at all.

I had never been great at making friends, but something about the newness of a new school had convinced me that this time would be different. We were all new to it: the school, the town, the teaching program. Surely my trouble connecting with people my whole life had been something about my hometown, some flaw in everyone else. Surely my new classmates, in a competitive grad school program for writing and literature, would immediately feel like friends.

Whatever instant connection I expected didn't happen. It seemed like everyone knew each other already or were roommates who had found each other on some housing listserv that I didn't even know about. One day into our teaching orientation there were couples forming already, the poets pairing up with the fiction writers. Everyone was older than me and sharing stories of the years they had spent teaching abroad, the books they already had published, the research they were looking forward to. I was the youngest person in the program and I hadn't done anything with my life yet. I didn't even drink, and with every social invitation I accepted I felt more and more inept, more deeply uncool, tagging along like someone's little sister.

I MET BUBBLES AT MAUREEN'S HOUSE, deep in the Massachusetts woods. She had been fostering him in his own bedroom, separate from her dogs, who Bubbles kept trying to fight. Sometimes she would lock the dogs in her bedroom and let Bubbles roam around the rest of the house, where he would follow her, nipping at her ankles for attention. *He's still learning how to accept love,* Maureen told me.

When I met Bubbles he was lounging on a cat tower by a window in his room, and when he heard us enter he meowed and stood up and stretched and then basked in the attention, purring as I scratched behind his ears. He was a black cat, but I hadn't expected the depth of his color: how gray he was under his armpits, how reddish brown the streaks down his back. He was enormously fluffy, the largest cat I had ever seen in person. I adopted him on the spot.

The next day, Maureen delivered him to my apartment in a carrier meant for a medium-size dog. He came with his cat tower, which I set up next to my bedroom window, an extra-large litter box, and a well-loved catnip toy. I had planned on renaming Bubbles. It was a silly name for a cat, and especially for a cat as wild and enormous as he was. I thought I would get to know him before settling on a new name, but instead I got to know him as Bubbles and it stuck. *Bubbly Wubbly,* I called him. *Bubblito. Mr. Bub.*

That first night, Bubbles was nervous and hid in my bathroom sink. I sat in the hall where I could see his glowing eyes through the doorway, and I tried to project all my gentleness and calmness and love toward him. Just having him there, I instantly felt an ease I hadn't felt in months, all my anxiety about school and friends and the future suddenly focused on this massive cat, on making sure he had a line of his favorite treats leading from the bathroom sink to the blanket I had placed for him on the couch, to lure him out when he was ready. He was a giant presence in my quiet apartment. Another beating heart.

THAT FIRST SEMESTER I FORCED myself to say yes to things, to attend social events where I didn't know anyone, to pore over the bus schedule until I figured out how to get to readings and parties and bars I had never heard of. I was friendly with everyone in my program but I hadn't clicked with anyone. Everyone else seemed to be meeting their soulmates, hosting big dinners, and launching new magazines together. I was constantly feeling one step behind.

Midsemester, there was a poetry reading half an hour away. Everyone I knew was going but somehow it also felt like no one I knew was going; like they were all going together and not with me. It was a public event but I didn't feel invited. I went anyway; I forced myself to. All I had to do, theoretically, was show up at this old warehouse that had been turned into a bookstore, sit in a little folding chair, and listen to people read poems.

Instead, I had my first dissociative episode. I had been staring at my hands and then suddenly I couldn't tell if they were my own hands, what hands were, where I was. I couldn't tell anymore if I was a person. Everyone was wearing outfits I didn't understand. The poetry seemed beyond me, and instead of feeling inspired I felt stupid, even more out of place, and I was sure that everyone there could tell that I was panicking.

I didn't even recognize the words as English. I was watching myself from outside my body, hovering somewhere near the ceiling. I didn't know anything about anxiety then, or how to ground myself, and instead I fixated on my ugly fingernails and then the cold breeze coming in from outside in the dark, and then I started to feel like everything around me was ominous, like I could die.

Part of it was impostor syndrome. I was an impostor academic and an impostor writer but also an impostor person; I didn't understand the most basic parts of how to interact with other people. I had been diagnosed with depression and anxiety as a teenager, but the clinical terms didn't seem to capture what I was feeling: my spiraling, my isolation, my deep fear that I was always on the brink of losing my mind. That something about me was fundamentally at odds with the world, that I couldn't see a future for myself. In class I tried to stay quiet. After class I walked home alone with the cold autumn air making my eyes water, and by the time I reached my apartment I couldn't even tell if I was crying.

———

I HAD IMAGINED HAVING a cat as a kind of corrective to isolation, a cure to my loneliness. Sometimes it worked. I could stay in bed all day, watching Bubbles watch the birds outside the window, and feel the warmth from his body against mine. I could call to him from anywhere in the apartment and he would answer with a heavy thud as he jumped down from wherever he was sleeping and ran to greet me.

But Bubbles never quite lost his wildness. Sometimes, in the middle of cuddling and purring, he would shake his head and stare at me, his eyes dilating, and then howl and bite, his teeth sinking into my forearm. There was no pattern to his behavior, no obvious trigger. It was like he was having flashbacks to his feral self, the days when he lived in the woods. Sometimes he would stalk me around the apartment, yowling, his eyes flashing, and more than once he successfully backed me into a corner while I quietly begged him to stop. *Bub*, I would say gently, trying to sound calm. *Bub, it's okay. It's just me. Please don't attack me. Bub.* My ankles started to show the scars of all the times he lunged at me.

My mom, when she visited, would tuck her pants into her socks so Bubbles couldn't bite her ankles, but when my dad came he would greet Bubbles before he even greeted me, sit down on the floor, and let Bubbles approach him. My dad sometimes stayed with Bub when I had to travel for conferences. He was a gentle man with a soft spot for black cats, underdogs, the misunderstood animals of the world. When he stayed with Bub he would text me updates each day, weirdly angled selfies of his face next to Bub's, with captions. *Two goofy guys!* one of the texts said. Bubbles, his giant face, his eyes narrowed in contentment.

When he wasn't biting, Bubbles was a sweet, enormous cat. He would settle onto my chest when I slept and I would delight in taking deep breaths, watching him rise and fall on top of me. He longed for affection in a way I found relatable. If I was away from the apartment for more than an hour I would come back to find him waiting at the door for me, his fluffy tail held high in the air as he pranced around my feet, like he couldn't believe I had actually come back.

Sometimes it felt like we weren't enough for each other, Bubbles and I, with his endless demands for attention and my ever-present loneliness. It was shocking to me that I could feel alone even with a cat purring next to me, that somehow a half-feral animal wasn't a suitable stand-in for a full community of people who cared.

I would think about this for years, like when the social isolation of pandemic quarantine led so many people to adopt companion animals for the first time. Or later still, when I would help people with all the cats they had accidentally hoarded, all the animals in their apartments they had collected for company, and I would learn again and again that the people prone to animal hoarding were so deeply lonely, living in complete isolation, often having lost many people they had loved.

My isolation and depression were twin forces, feeding each other. I'm certain that Bubbles saved my life. In my most critical moments I would remind myself that I had to stay alive for Bubbles, that no one else would tolerate his wild love the way I did. He was a living presence that I desperately needed, a creature who would greet me at the door. But he didn't save me from sitting up late at night sobbing, wanting to have deep, yearning conversations with other people, with other humans. Bubbles would snore in his sleep beside me. I wanted so badly for him to be everything I needed.

I WOULD HAVE SAID, that first year of grad school, that my deepest insecurity was about the coursework, about my intellect, about my inability to keep up with a demanding program. Maybe the problem was my work ethic, the way everyone else seemed to spend their free time reading dense books of literary theory and I spent mine binge-watching every season of *30 Rock*, keeping the characters, with their safe, familiar voices, constantly in the background of my brain to quiet my anxiety. How was everyone else doing it? How did everyone else already know all the academic jargon, all the words I had never heard before? In classes I kept a running list of new words to look up, and back at my apartment I would google them and still not understand what they meant.

I knew that the only way to succeed in academia was to be exceptional, and exceptionalism turned out to be a lonely thing to believe in. Only one of us could get the coveted assistantship that would pay the bills for a semester; only one of us could win the year's teaching award. Only one of us would get the tenure-track job at the end of all of it, and this wasn't an exaggeration: there was something like one tenure-track job for every three hundred new PhDs. It was a simple fact of capitalism, an open secret, that most of us would not succeed. All the program brochures I had pored over before deciding on a school had touted their literary communities, their academic mentors, the shining photos of diverse groups of students, with their glasses and their laptops, gathered in beautiful brick rooms. In reality, any sense of community felt antithetical to all of it. There could only be one of us.

I believed in rugged individualism and I believed in it fiercely: doing it all myself, never asking for help. Wasn't I here, in this PhD program, because I had beat out so many other people? Hadn't I escaped my hometown because I had been the best? Someday, I was sure, I would look back at all my years of lonely suffering and know they had gotten me to the top. I believed that.

―――――

MY MUCH DEEPER INSECURITY, which I tried not to think about and which instead came out in wailing sobs late at night, was that I had no one to call in an emergency. By the end of that first semester it seemed like everyone had formed friendships so intense they would die for each other. We were all making poverty-level wages but my classmates seemed to me to be living a romanticized version of poverty, where someone's car broke down and it became a funny story, how all their roommates trekked through the snow to rescue them. Or they were all broke but scraping by, sharing Sunday dinners together, surviving on communal lentils and beans. One colleague had emergency surgery and everyone rallied around her, bringing her flowers and delivering meals to her apartment while she recovered, and I couldn't quiet the nagging voice in my head that said: *No one would do that for you.*

My life felt like a long series of emergencies, and I went through each one alone. They were mostly small things: my car would break down, my plumbing would go out, I would accidentally lock myself out of my apartment. Silly things, the kind of things you quickly call a friend for and they come to the rescue. But each time I would find myself scrolling through my phone, checking my contacts, thinking about who I could call. And each time I would start to feel a sneaking sense of shame, an unsettling suspicion that perhaps I had no one. That I was the kind of person who would always have no one.

Instead I had Bubbles. I poured myself into caring for him, making his life as perfect as I could. He slept on my desk, where I studied and read, his body stretched across my keyboard. I spent every Saturday grading undergraduate essays and Bubbles helped, chewing the tip of my pen as I wrote comments in the margins. He was afraid of the rain, and when clouds rolled in, he would hide in the bathtub, and I would climb in there with him. *It's okay*, I would tell him, and I would play music from my phone that echoed off the shower tile and drowned out the sound of the rain. I would cover Bubbles with a blanket, brush the big beardy fluff of his chin. I would wish, in a way I couldn't put into words, that someone would do the same for me. That I could admit to anyone that I was scared, that someone would sit with me and speak quiet reassurances.

It's okay, I would tell Bub. *I'm here with you.*

———

BUBBLES ONCE BIT A COP. It would become the story I'd tell about him for years. I had started to learn his patterns, had started to realize that I needed to give him attention the second I stepped in the door or else he would get bitey, as if he had to be reminded at regular intervals that he was a well-loved domestic cat or he would revert to being feral. Most of the time I was good at this, putting my books down every half hour to kiss him gently on his giant head. When I got home, I would drop my bags and immediately lie down on the floor, right there inside the door, the itchy student-housing carpet pressing into my neck. Bubbles loved this. He would sniff my shoes and then work his way up my body, purring, burrowing his face into my armpits, welcoming me home. *Yes*, he would seem to say. *I am full of love. I am not a wild animal.*

That night a man followed me home from the coffee shop where I had been trying to write a paper. He had seen me there, watched me leave, watched to see which bus I had gotten on. He had run to his car—a red sedan, I still remember—and followed the bus, slowed at each bus stop, waited to see if I was one of the figures who stepped off in the dark. He watched me walk from the bus stop to my apartment, and, as I was reaching for my keys to let myself in, he pulled up outside my door and said: *Hello. I've been watching you.*

I called the police. I sat panicking inside my apartment, unsure if the red sedan was still out there, if the man was in his car or somewhere in the shadows outside my door. I was scared, and all my scariest moments were tinged with the shame of not having anyone to call for comfort. Bubbles was winding himself around my feet, welcoming me home. I was distracted. I somehow had not been able to give the 911 operator a description of the man—when I tried to picture him there was just blank panic in my mind—and she had chastised me for this. *Why didn't you call sooner?* she asked, even though I had only been home for five minutes.

Ten minutes later there was a police officer searching the perimeter of my little yard, making sure my windows were locked. *There's not really much else we can do*, he told me. He was an intimidating presence in my apartment, standing in my living room. Bubbles walked over to us, his paws silent on the carpet. He sniffed the cop's pant leg, seemed to consider for a moment, and then stretched his neck out and—almost in slow motion—bit him hard on the calf.

The man in the red sedan followed me home twice more after that. I didn't call anyone. I just went inside and sat with Bubbles.

———

THAT GRAD SCHOOL APARTMENT was on the first floor, with a grassy backyard where I sometimes saw rabbits. Bubbles would chatter his teeth by the window, his wild side coming out, and I would crouch down next to him and we would watch the rabbits together. I shared one wall with neighbors. When I moved in there was a woman living in the next-door apartment, but I never met her. She never seemed to go outside, and I only ever heard her late at night, crying in what must have been her bathroom. At some point I realized she could probably hear me crying, too.

When that neighbor moved out, a couple moved in. They were my age. They knocked on my door their first week in town to introduce themselves, and they met Bubbles, who regarded them warily from a distance. *He bites*, I told them, and they seemed charmed.

Matt and Krista brought me cookies after that, and every time I saw them outside they asked how Bubbles was. They strung up a hammock in the yard and invited me to use it. When they played music, they would text to ask if it was too loud. They were the platonic ideal of neighbors, the exact kind I had hoped for, and it was my fault we never became friends. They would invite me over for dinner and I would decline. They would have friends over to play badminton in the yard and they would playfully harass me to join, calling through my screen windows to get my attention. *Leave Bub-*

bles for five minutes! they would say. *Come hang out!* Their friends would be grilling hamburgers and tossing Frisbees right outside my window and I would hide in the bedroom with Bub.

I went next door to their apartment only once, when they invited me again for dinner and I couldn't come up with an excuse quickly enough. Their apartment was the exact inverse of mine, a mirror image, and we owned all the same cheap furniture from Target: the same full-length mirror, the same plastic drawers in the bathroom. Krista had made chili and Matt had arranged a buffet of toppings—sour cream and green onions and cheese and chips—and as we ate they asked friendly questions about my graduate program, about what I was teaching. I can't remember if I asked them any questions in return. I spent most of the evening either complaining or trying to seem normal. Even though it was exactly what I had imagined—kind neighbors to share dinners with, an escape from the isolation of my tiny life—I hated it. I didn't have the energy to care about Matt and Krista; I had no space in my brain for curiosity about other people. Their life seemed so wholly different from mine that it didn't seem worth even trying to comprehend. I was focused with absolute singularity on survival, and my survival was selfish; it didn't care who suffered for it.

I didn't understand then how much I had constructed my own loneliness, how I protected it like a fortress. I romanticized my isolation, steeped in my sadness. The only life I truly spent time thinking about was my own, and everything about my world encouraged this: the long hours I spent preparing to teach classes, the low wages that left me constantly stressed, all the emphasis on my responsibility to build my own career if I ever wanted to make enough money to afford rent without relying on student loans. My life felt precarious and the precarity made it feel impossible to be generous. What did I even have to give?

I wanted belonging to be something I could inherit, something I could step into fully formed. I imagined community as a space I could passively inhabit. It would be so many years before I learned that community was an action, something we build and rebuild and contribute to. That belonging is something we invent.

———

AFTER FOUR YEARS I LEFT school without a degree. My life wasn't what I had imagined, my mental health was worsening, and the future felt impossible. I moved across the country to Tucson, a place I had chosen for how far away it was from Massachusetts, where I had lived my whole life. I wasn't scared at all of moving somewhere new. If anything, it was an excuse: if I was new in town, of course I would have no one. It was much harder to have no one in a place I had lived for years.

The question was whether Bubbles could come with me.

Bubbles was anxious and carsick just on ten-minute drives to the vet; I couldn't imagine driving him cross-country with me. *Do you want to go on a road trip?* I asked him, and he blinked and stretched out across my bed. I never used a singsongy voice with him, never baby-talked. I spoke to him the way I would a roommate. A friend.

I knew he wouldn't do well on the trip. I knew I couldn't leave him behind.

When I told my dad I was leaving school and moving to Tucson, he offered before I could ask: *Been thinking about the big move*, he texted. *If Bub needs a more permanent cat sitter, you know he's welcome here.*

Bubbles and my dad turned out to be soulmates. My parents had just divorced, and my mom had kept their cat; my dad was suddenly living alone, without a cat, for the first time in decades. It was what Bub was good at: being a new presence in the life of someone feeling acutely alone.

Bubbles lived four more years, in a rambling old house that my dad had essentially converted, room by room, into a cat resort. There were ramps from the floor to the ceiling, little cat paths affixed to the walls, steps that led to cat towers and favorite chairs and soft beds next to a woodstove. Bub was mostly sweet with my dad—he thrived with so much space and such a regular routine—but occasionally I would get texts late at night, pictures of my dad's hands covered in bite marks, Bubbles glowering in the background. *Biting hard*, the texts would say. *Total jerk. I love him.*

THE ENDING IS THAT BUBBLES DIED. Or it wasn't an ending; it was the start. At nine years old, after many months of treatment for lymphoma, Bubbles stopped breathing in my dad's arms on a hot mid-August day. It was the same day I moved in to the house in Poets Square.

The ending is also that for years after that I thought maybe Bubbles had known more than me. That maybe somehow, across the country and across dimensions, Bubbles had been sending me a message: *Here are a bunch more semi-feral animals for you to love.* My dad grieved deeply for Bub, seeing his spirit in every kind of wildness: in the woods, in the foxes that walked his neighborhood, in every insect that appeared at his window, hovering on the other side of the screen. I saw Bub in every cat who showed up at my door needing help. *Message received, Bubblito*, I would say. And as I drove cat after cat to the vet, I would remember all the nights I spent sobbing into Bubbles's fur, feeling so desperately alone. I remembered the way he would lick my face when I cried, although he rarely groomed himself. Bub had always seemed to be missing some essential knowledge about how to be a cat, like he had skipped some lessons as a kitten, and it was one of the things that had endeared me to him from the start. *Neither of us know what we're doing*, I used to whisper to him, and he would purr, his deep hearty rumbling vibrating back into my bones.

Sometimes when I think about loneliness I still think about Bubbles, how thoroughly he defined a time in my life. How much I relied on him, his big animal heaviness on my chest, how he would bound toward the door to greet me. How much easier it was to tell myself that he was the only thing I needed than it was to confront even the idea of needing other people. How messy and essential it is to need.

Bubbles, my enormous and only friend, into whom I had poured all my affection. The giant signifier of my isolation. He died the same day we moved in to our house and for so many years it would feel significant, like my own self-centeredness had created him, like my loneliness had kept him alive. Sometimes I think the best way to remember Bubbles is to save other cats, as many of them as I can, all the half-feral and aggressive cats, the cats emerging from the woods starving and unloved, the cats wild and biting. But I remember Bubbles most when I'm with other people, when friends text me just to check in, when I drop off soup for someone who is sick. When a card shows up in the mail from an old grad school classmate, with a sweet note about the cats and a gift card to PetSmart. All the people I would come to rely on, all the ways I would shed my self-reliance. I didn't know it then, everything that would come after Bubbles, everything I would learn from the way he needed love and announced it to the world.

IN POETS SQUARE, WHEN I MADE my cats an Instagram account, a woman named Katy commented on one of my posts to say that she lived in my neighborhood and loved cats, if I ever needed help. I invited her over to meet the cats, and then she fed them for me for a weekend when I was out of town, and then we kept texting. I couldn't stop thinking about it, how simple it had been: how Katy had walked over to the house and now she was sitting in my carport with me, and we were talking about cats and then we were talking about the neighborhood, and where we had lived before that, and how we both ended up here and what we had struggled with and what we hoped for, and then Katy was my friend, an actual friend, and when I got sick later that year she was dropping off dinner at my door, offering to walk my dog.

I met Gerald because he adopted a kitten I saved from a hoarding situation. The kitten had been kept inside a filthy hamster cage and now instead he lived with Gerald, and years later when my car broke down Gerald was the one to rescue me from the side of the road. I met Annie because she also fed stray cats, and years later when I locked myself out of my house, she was the one with a spare key. I met Isaac and Shannon because they also ran an Instagram account about cats, and for years after that Isaac would listen to the police scanner and text me any time he heard about a car accident with a vehicle description that matched mine. *You okay?* he would text. *Just checking in!*

I met Abby because she fostered the sick kittens that I dug out from piles of garbage, and Rachael because she was also a volunteer cat trapper, and Angéline because she worked at the local animal shelter, and then years passed and we were all having dinner together, all the time, and texting each other when we were sick or sad or anxious or in love. We hosted parties and potlucks and when we were depressed, we cleaned each other's houses. We made care packages. We showed up.

I met friends when I didn't even mean to, and for the longest time I couldn't understand the difference, why I had struggled for so long and then suddenly I didn't: I had thirty cats and thirty friends, a whole community, an endless list of people I could call in an emergency. Maybe it was that there was less competition in cat rescue; we weren't all striving for a single job. Maybe it was that we were all there to help each other, genuinely, because we were all in the trenches of seeing animals suffer and it was impossible to do it alone. Maybe it was me. Maybe I had taken my whole self-absorbed heart, all those years of focusing only on myself, and let thirty cats turn it entirely inside out.

Mothering

I was at the spay and neuter clinic when someone wished me a happy Mother's Day.

It wasn't clear whether she was making a joke—maybe referring to the cats I was dropping off as my kids?—or whether I had reached an age at which I was assumed by default to be a mother. I realized later that there would be no reason for a stranger to joke about this—she didn't know I had thirty cats and no uterus—but it felt just as absurd to think that anyone could look at me and assume I'm a mother.

On Instagram, people have been referring to me as the cats' mom. *Hello Cat Mom!* people say in the comments. Or, worse, they call me *Mommy*. Sometimes *Meowmy*, which disgusts me. I feel a visceral discomfort about all of this, about anything that assumes I'm anyone's mom. *Aww, she loves her mommy*, the comments say when little calico MK accepts a treat from me.

I really don't think of myself as their mom, I keep responding. *I'm more like their Large Pal.*

WHEN I MET MK SHE was already pregnant. I didn't know it. Maybe I could have guessed, by how strangely proportioned she was, how tiny her triangular face appeared above her taut belly. She was feral: tiny and wild-eyed, keeping thirty feet away from me, eating her meals by stealing a mouthful and retreating, swallowing hard while her eyes darted all over. When she ran she kept her body low to the ground, her belly getting bigger and bigger until it brushed against the dirt.

MK was my favorite from the first time I saw her. I think I'm not supposed to have favorites among the cats—like a mom with her kids—but I couldn't help it. It was something about her intensity, about how enormous her eyes would get, how expressive her face. She was an anxious cat, pure high-strung neuroticism, and she had been living in survival mode for so long. The black mask across her eyes made her look like a bandit.

I adored her.

When I realized MK was pregnant—when her belly was the size of a watermelon—I thought: *That's it, then. I will make a place for her to have her babies, and she will have them.* I don't know what I thought would come after that, this tiny wild cat raising feral babies in my yard. I didn't know then that you can spay a pregnant cat, that you can terminate the pregnancy.

Some vets won't do a pregnant spay. Some rescuers won't recommend it; some won't even talk about it. But the truth is that there's nowhere for those babies to go, not even in the best circumstances, and in stray malnourished cats who have never had any vet care, pregnancy and birth have so many complications: stillborn kittens, deadly uterine infections, so many things that can go wrong. It's hard to think of something sadder than starving kittens, but for me it's their starving moms: the haunted, hollow look they get in their eyes. They're just babies themselves. They're acting on pure instinct, all evolution, to keep their kittens alive.

When MK gave birth she chose our neighbors' yard, on the other side of our wall, where I couldn't see her. I was up early that morning, before the sun rose, and when I put out breakfast for all the cats, MK didn't show up. *I hope she's not giving birth right now*, I thought. It was cold enough that I could see my breath.

―――――

AT AGE FIVE I HAD my first major surgery. Something about my kidneys, some things that just never formed right. I stayed in the pediatric intensive care unit for a week.

I was an anxious kid, shy to the point of panic attacks, and the most horrifying part of the hospital wasn't the needles or the incisions or the medications that made me feel itchy inside my own skin but the strangers: new nurses and doctors and attendants entering my room, trying to make small talk, touching my body. It terrified me, made me feel tiny in my hospital bed, to have to face these people. I was usually the kid hiding behind my mom's legs, letting her do the talking for me, and now—in a hospital room, hooked up to tubes and too painful to move—there was nowhere to hide.

Once, a nurse complimented the stuffed dog I had just received as a get-well-soon gift, and I clutched the dog like she was going to take it away. *Have you named her?* the nurse asked. *What's her name?*

I stayed silent. I wish I could explain now how terrifying I found people at the time, how impossible it felt to speak to a stranger. It was an all-encompassing fear, a terror I can't understand as an adult.

She looks cuddly, the nurse said. *Is her name Cuddles?*

I nodded to make her go away, and she did.

Cuddles became my prized possession, even as a teenager. I used to tell it like a funny story—*I couldn't even answer a question! I would say yes to anything to make people go away!*—but now it's sad, to think about the things I spent my life saying yes to, to think about how many days of my childhood I spent terrified, hospitalized, my nervous system never resting.

My mom was in the hospital with me the whole time, and as a kid I never questioned it—whether that was standard, what she was giving up to be there. Of course she was there; she was my protector, and also my interpreter when I could speak only in anxious squeaks, when I had a speech impediment severe enough that I couldn't say my own name.

In the pediatric ICU, my mom spent nights on a chair in the corner of my room, and then, after a few restless nights, machines beeping as she tried to sleep upright, the nurses let her know that there was a room down the hall where parents could sleep. A little quieter. Real beds. Or cots, at least. I was too young to understand any of it—how tired my mom was, and how scared; the absolute fatigue in her eyes; how painful her own body was from staying up twisted in strange positions, trying to get comfortable on a sanitized armchair—and I asked her not to go. I begged her. *Don't go to the room down the hall. Please. Please, Mom. Stay here in the room with me.*

And she did. She stayed in my room, upright and restless, resisting sleep each time my machines beeped in the dark.

THERE WAS HOWLING OUTSIDE. I knew all the cats' sounds by then, the sounds of fighting and mating, the little skirmishes versus the serious fights, the sound of an injured cat. The howling coming from outside my bedroom window was none of those. It sounded like a cat had been mortally wounded. It was a chilling noise, and when I heard it I stood up almost involuntarily, ran to the window to check.

It was MK. She was in the front yard, pacing and searching, unable to sit still. She was yowling, screaming, letting sounds out of her mouth that I couldn't have guessed she contained. She was tiny and wild and completely undone, frantic, the fur along her spine puffed up. She was wailing.

Her stomach wasn't a watermelon anymore. She looked like she had been deflated.

I would learn later that MK had given birth next door. The neighbors had found her kitten—just one—and, assuming it had been abandoned on a cold morning, brought it inside. They were doing a good job. They had the kitten on a little heating pad, feeding him formula from an eyedropper. The kitten was okay, orange and white, impossibly small with a plump little belly. His eyes were still closed.

But they didn't know the baby was MK's. They didn't know MK was outside, searching. Tracing her path around the yard with her nose to the ground, throwing her head back and crying. She was desperate, sniffing everything: each rock, each toy, each bed. She sniffed the trash can and the fence and the trees, trotting frantically toward anything small enough that it could have been a kitten, putting her face desperately against it, howling: *Are you my baby? Did I birth you?*

She was all instinct, all hormones, searching for something to mother. Her kitten was tucked safely inside a dish towel inside our neighbors' house, rocked to sleep in front of a space heater, where her howling couldn't reach him.

MY FIRST SURGERY FAILED. We didn't learn this until a year later, at follow-up testing, when I was six years old. The doctor explained to my mom that the problem had not only returned in my left kidney but was now causing problems in my right kidney, too. I wasn't paying attention until he said the word *operation,* which I recognized, and after that my mom and I sat in the waiting room and cried. *We have to do it again*, she said, and I knew everything that meant: new incisions, new needles, new strangers. The huge fish tanks in the waiting room glowed murky and dark.

For my second surgery we were in some kind of hospital suite that included a bathroom with a shower, and I remember my mom being excited about this, and me not understanding why. This unit also had a little activity room down the hall, and when I was well enough to move from my bed to a wheelchair my mom would push me down there to string little beads into bracelets. I made one for myself and one for my mom and we wore them together, holding hands in my hospital bed.

I remember being in pain and holding Cuddles tight against my belly while I coughed. The medicine they gave me for pain made me nauseous, and the nausea made me panic. The little plastic bins that hospitals give you when you might puke were shaped like kidneys, and as a kid I thought they were made specifically for me.

I only remember my mom showering in the hospital once. I

begged her not to. I was seven years old and still barely capable of existing; I was missing half of first grade for surgery and in school I still cried every day. *I will take the fastest shower anyone has ever taken*, my mom told me, and I believed her but knew it wouldn't be fast enough. She made sure I had water and crackers, and my meds were up to date, my IV dripping, no nurses due to check on me in the next five minutes. She gave me the button that would call the nurses' station, in case anything happened and I needed to summon help, but I knew I wouldn't use it. And then she stepped into the bathroom five feet away.

I got nauseous. Immediately. The deep, twisting kind of nausea, the full-body shivers, the feeling in my diaphragm that I couldn't control. I panicked. It wasn't that I thought my mom could do anything to stop it; it was that I had never, in my seven years on earth, had to experience any kind of pain alone. I had no mechanism for it. The only way I knew to get through pain was to pour it into my mother, to let her absorb every bit of it, every unpleasantness, and this is probably why I reached age twenty-five without knowing how to process any of my own emotions. I never learned to self-soothe. But at seven, in pediatric intensive care, terrified of strangers and with too many tubes coming out of my body, my belly cut up in fresh five-inch incisions, I was about to throw up. I could feel it rising in my throat and I didn't know what to do. I screamed for my mom.

The nurses heard me first, even though I hadn't pressed the call button—wouldn't, because the nurses were not who I wanted beside me—and when they entered my room, I wouldn't tell them what was wrong. I wouldn't talk. Couldn't talk. I just cried, just heaved and screamed, and the nurses ran panicking around me trying to figure out how to help. They fetched my mom, dragged her out of the first shower she'd had in a week, and she was wrapping a bathrobe around herself and squeezing thick bubbly suds from her hair when she rushed to my side, and it was only then—only when my mom was next to me, able to interpret my pain and then absorb it, channel all of my panic and screaming into herself—that I said: *I feel like I'm gonna throw up.*

And then I did. I threw up all over my mom.

———

WE CALLED GEORGIE THE BABY of the cat colony, but she was only a few months younger than MK. She was a fluffy little tuxedo cat, black and white, almost a year old. She liked to sleep in the garden, in a cluster of flowering vines, and if a mosquito or moth got too close to her face she would eat it, just chomp it out of midair and chew it lazily as the vines curled around her head like a crown. She was a relaxed cat, always napping, the antithesis of MK's neuroticism. She was spayed young. She never had babies.

That's what Georgie was doing—lounging in the leaves, shielding her eyes from the sun with a tufty white paw thrown over her face—when MK found her.

MK, still searching for her baby, desperate for something to mother, saw Georgie and visibly relaxed. She shook off her shoulders, went nearly limp with relief. She seemed to think: *There she is. My enormous newborn. My giant infant kitten.*

She ran to her.

MK licked Georgie hard across the forehead and paused—*Yes, yes, my kitten!*—and then picked her up by the scruff of her neck. Georgie didn't protest. MK dragged her across the yard, into a bed in our carport, and when Georgie got up to run away, MK grabbed her again. *Get back here, you feisty newborn*, she seemed to say, and it went like this for ten minutes: MK dragging a full-grown cat back to bed and then practically sitting on her, insisting that this was her kitten, and Georgie confused but having fun, thinking it was a game, trotting a few steps away and waiting for MK to follow.

I was watching from a window. I couldn't tell if I should intervene, had no idea what the protocol was for an adult cat mistaking another adult cat for her kitten. I didn't know where the actual kitten was, didn't know how to help MK, my neurotic little heart, as she had searched and suffered and wailed. MK's relief as she trotted anxious circles around Georgie was palpable, her little cat body trilling with excited relief at having found her kitten: *My baby, yes, you are safe, you are safe with me.* As I watched, Georgie relented, sprawled out in the bed, and MK started licking her, somewhat harshly, across her whole body. The way moms do.

MK looked pleased with herself, having finally wrangled her enormous infant into bed and now cleaning her thoroughly, finally catching up on all the mothering her animal instincts were imploring her to do. Georgie looked content, not sure what was happening but okay with it. When I went outside MK stood up and hissed. *Get back*, she seemed to say, putting herself physically between me and Georgie. *This is my child and I birthed her.*

I backed off.

I WAS TWENTY-THREE WHEN MY MOM was diagnosed with cancer. It started in her tonsils, and it kept coming back; her most recent surgery was to remove most of her tongue. I was there. I was on the other side of it that time, watching someone I love rolled away on a white bed, waiting hours until the surgeon came out to talk to me, to say it was worse than he expected. My mom couldn't talk when she woke up. Her mouth was a pool of blood. She was trying to say something, opening her mouth and then closing it again, looking panicked, half conscious, and I was leaning closer and closer to her, trying and failing to understand what she was saying. She made a tiny noise and I was desperate to translate it. She was saying: *pain*.

Seeing my mom go through multiple rounds of cancer treatment unhinged something in me. The first time, I fully believed she was going to die. It was true then that she was no longer the mom I had always had, that that version of her was gone. I spent days grieving her like she was already dead, and then confronting the fact of her still alive, trying to reconcile my dead mom with my living mom with the version of my mom who was so sick, so thin, so vulnerable and weak. For months, I cried for someone who was sitting right next to me. Years later I would learn the term *anticipatory grief* and it made me feel less insane to learn about it, to have a vocabulary for what I was feeling.

But that last time, the time with the tongue, broke something in me more permanently. Her recovery was so long and I was living so far away, flying across the country to be with her. She couldn't talk at all, those first few weeks, and she communicated by writing notes on a little pad of paper. *Did they get all of it?* her first note after surgery read. I nodded yes. *And the lymph nodes?* Yes. *How long is my scar?* The scar was a long semicircle around her neck, like someone had tried to decapitate her. *Not that long*, I told her.

It was exhausting for her to write the notes. We mostly sat quietly. Every hour or so she would blink her eyes open and write *pain* or <u>*pain*</u> or *PAIN* and I would summon the nurses, call for doctors, and they would cluster around her to figure out what else they could give her, what they could push through the vein of her IV. It was winter, and the view out her hospital window was Worcester, Massachusetts, the steep hills making the houses look stacked on top of each other, the mill buildings sitting empty with their broken windows. I felt desolate. Hollowed.

My mom kept closing her eyes and opening them, kept trying to move her mouth and wincing with her whole body. She looked scared. The notebook passed between us was just pages of pain. On one page, in handwriting recognizable as hers but crooked and weak, she wrote: *I'm glad you're here with me.*

———

FEMALE CATS WITH NEW BABIES are the easiest to trap, because they'll do anything to get to their kittens. If they're scared of traps, scared of people, completely feral, not food-motivated—it doesn't matter. They'll do anything.

You find the kittens, with their tiny high-pitched cries, and put them in a carrier at the back end of the trap, where normally the food would go. The other end is an open door. Mama cat will hear the cries and she'll circle the trap, listening, sniffing. Sometimes she gets frantic and it's heartbreaking—you can tell how scared she is, how terrified of the trap, and sometimes it seems like she knows it's a trap, knows exactly what will happen when she steps in. But it doesn't matter. She has to follow those kitten cries; she can't help it. And then she steps in and the door closes behind her.

Sometimes I even use YouTube for this, play recorded sounds of kittens to make a mother cat emerge. It's baffling to me, the way an animal can respond to a sound almost unwillingly, the way instinct takes over. Probably human moms are the same. Aren't new mothers somehow in sync with their babies, somehow attuned to the exact pitch of their cries? Didn't my mom sprint from her shower when I screamed?

This is how I tried to trap MK, that morning after she gave birth.

I tried first with her kitten—her actual kitten, a just-born orange and white boy, curled like a comma and crying. When I found him inside with the neighbors, asleep in a shoebox, I brought him back to MK. She was so curious about him at first—*A tiny thing? My baby?*—but it was too late. When he cried in his carrier MK only looked confused. She heard the cries, registered them in her little cat brain, but something wasn't right. She wasn't trying to find him. Each time he cried, MK ran to Georgie. It didn't make sense, but maybe mothering never does. Her maternal wires had gotten crossed.

I found a rescue to take in the kitten, that tiny day-old thing, where a cat who had just given birth adopted him into her litter. She nursed him and licked him hard down his back, cleaning him, making him smell like her own.

In the driveway, we tried again to trap MK, this time with Georgie in the carrier. I thought, *There's no way this will work*—not MK, who had eluded traps for a month now, terrified of anything new in her environment, so hungry but still not enough to brave a metal cage for a meal. Georgie meowed, just once, in the carrier. And MK ran, low on her haunches, sniffing and pawing around, trying to find the cat the same size as her that she somehow thought was her baby. She was suddenly desperate again—*That's my baby, my baby is in there*—and she walked right into the trap.

I took her straight to the vet to get spayed. *You will never have to do this again*, I told her, and it was a promise.

CARING FOR MY MOM AFTER her surgery was the worst thing I've done. I thought constantly about my own surgeries, all my childhood illnesses, if it had been horrible for her. If she had ever resented it, if she had stayed up all night sick with the knowledge of it all, how barbaric the treatments can be. As a kid I had considered myself an extension of my mother and I wondered if she felt the same way, if she ever felt my kidneys misfiring in her own body, the pain of the incisions low across my belly.

I had flown across the country, back to my hometown, to be there for her surgery, and after a few weeks it was a deep relief to be able to board a flight, to leave her recovery a few states away. Every night, I dreamed that criminals had kidnapped her, were holding her hostage, and I couldn't get there in time to help.

In the years before, I had taken my mom to chemo and radiation, had been with her when she had her feeding tube placed and then removed. I used to drive her car while she rode in the front seat, nauseous and coughing, and pulled over every few hundred feet so she could vomit in the snow. She was so dehydrated those days that the skin on the back of her hands looked like paper. She lost her hair, started wearing thickly knitted winter hats. She looked like a paper doll version of herself, faded and flat.

I spent my time in hospitals and doctors' offices, pharmacies and waiting rooms, pushing my mom in a wheelchair down white hospital hallways, and all the time felt like a little kid playing dress-up, like someone had taken the game too seriously and I wanted it to stop. When my mom couldn't talk, I had to talk for her, had to fetch nurses when her hospital machines beeped, had to argue on the phone with doctors who wouldn't give her more painkillers. I wanted to beg someone to end the game, to let me take my costume off and go back to being a child. *I'm not her mom*, I wanted to say. *She's supposed to be the mom.*

GEORGIE'S REAL MOM WAS MONKEY, who looked just like MK and was probably her sister. Monkey hadn't been much of a mom to Georgie. I only knew this from our neighbors, who had seen Monkey give birth before we had moved in. *She didn't seem interested in being a mom*, the neighbor told me. *She wouldn't nurse the kittens.*

Monkey hadn't been a good mom because she had been starving, scared, exhausted. Trying to survive. When I met her a few months later she would eat in frenzied bursts, growling, ready to fight for her food. Her body just didn't have enough to also nurse kittens. Her instincts said *survive*, and she did.

Georgie survived, too, raised not by Monkey but by a bowl of milk, by a well-intentioned neighbor, by the rest of the cats, all thirty of them, who all seemed to share an agreement to be nice to Georgie. To be gentle with the baby. She was raised by a gang of feral street cats, grew up rough-and-tumble, tagged along with the bigger cats to find food.

But maybe Georgie was missing something maternal in her life when MK decided that she was a newborn again. Georgie thrived in it, nuzzling into MK as they slept, blinking contentedly as MK groomed her long fur. She got some kind of comfort from it, nursing from a cat who wasn't her mom, falling asleep safe, knowing MK was ready to defend her from anything. MK had needed someone to mother and Georgie had needed a mom, and they found each other.

ONE OF OUR NEIGHBORS CALLS all cats *kids* and after years I still haven't gotten used to it. *Thank you for taking care of all the neighborhood kids*, she said the first time I met her, and for a moment I had a vision of myself as the friendly neighborhood mom with a nice backyard where all the neighbor kids hung out. The mom who always had snacks, the house where everyone gathered. I pictured myself helping with homework, handing out Halloween candy.

I mean it, the neighbor said, mistaking my pause for some kind of humility. *Those kids are lucky to have you.* She meant the cats, of course. Maybe she was right.

MY MOST RECENT SURGERY was a hysterectomy. I had ovarian cysts and when my doctor started talking about all the ways to make sure I could still have kids someday, I said: *I don't want that*. I hadn't meant to say it, but it was true. The doctor just shrugged and said: *Well, even easier. Do you wanna take the whole thing out?*

Six weeks later I was recovering with four new incisions across my abdomen, intersecting with all my childhood scars. My first day home from the hospital I told Tim that I felt better than expected, and I lowered myself carefully into bed and slept for hours. When I woke up, I realized that the painkillers had worn off and everything hurt and I was helpless. I felt like a child again, frozen, screaming for my mom. Tim found me in bed, my eyes full of tears, and I couldn't explain why I was crying.

Instead of narcotics for pain, my surgeon had given me a pain pump: a tube that cut through my skin near my groin and delivered numbing medication directly to the most painful parts of my body. In some places I could tell it was working. I could push my fingers into the soft skin of my stomach and feel nothing at all.

I learned to feed the cats without moving my torso, without bending near my incisions. I could carry one bowl of food at a time and bend at the knees, lowering myself, keeping the top of my body straight as I put the food down. I did this again and again, setting out two bowls of food, and then four, and then six. Lowering myself, the tubes of the pain pump tucked neatly against my body, with fresh bowls of water, with treats.

Tim kept telling me to stop, to wait until he got home from work so he could take care of it. So he could take care of me. But the cats couldn't understand the tubes coming out of my body, the organs I had given up. I tended to the cats obsessively, ignoring the painful pulling of my stitches when I bent down to pick up their empty bowls. MK had learned by then to wait at the door for her dinner. I couldn't say no.

MK had climbed trees, searched the very top branches, as if somehow she might have lost her newborn up there. She had searched under bushes, under our cars. The pain in her little cat screams. *I have all this care to give*, she was screaming. *I have all this care to give.*

———

ONCE, MY MOM AND I counted how many surgery scars we have between us. Once, I cataloged everyone who has ever cared for me in the wake of surgery. My mom, all those childhood times. My ex-boyfriend, when I had my gallbladder taken out in an emergency. Tim, and then Tim again, and then Tim again. The time I had my gallbladder removed my mom wanted to be there, wanted to fly across the country to make sure someone was making me chicken soup as I recovered, but she couldn't. That was the same week she learned her cancer was back.

———

NOW ALL OF MY FRIENDS are having babies. Every time someone announces their pregnancy, I feel a vague sense of loss I can't quite parse.

I have all this care to give.

———

I WOULD ADOPT THIS CAT AS my legal child if I could, I wrote once about MK. It was a caption for a photo, one I had bribed MK into posing for by holding a treat in one hand and my camera in the other and scooting closer to her on my butt, inch by inch, across the gravel driveway, trying not to scare her. In the picture she looks plush and too perfect to be real, her white paws somehow round like a stuffed animal's. Her eyes are so expressive that they're almost cartoonish and in the photo she's looking past the camera at me, her eyes round with curiosity, her face a combination of wariness and wanting.

After she was spayed, I took care of MK like she was my child. I don't know how to cook, couldn't make chicken soup if I tried, and this has always horrified my mom. *What if you have kids one day?* she used to ask. *What if they get sick?* But I can scoop a can of cat food into a bowl; I can smash it with the back of a fork and add water until it's soupy. I can crush an antibiotic pill and mix it in; I can sprinkle the top with treats like a garnish. I can serve it to MK in the driveway, on all fours, pushing the bowl slowly toward her and then sitting back, watching, as she sniffs it. I can make sure she eats it all.

Do you need anything else? I would ask her, and she would blink at me from her bed, her belly shaved, her spay incision already scarring over.

After MK was spayed, Georgie started nursing from her. Every day, every few hours, like an actual newborn kitten, pushing her head against MK's belly and suckling. When I shared this online everyone wanted an explanation, something biological or behavioral, for why a pair of unrelated adult cats would do this. I didn't have an explanation. Georgie had been an independent cat, a fully grown adult, and then MK found her and loved her and Georgie thought: *Oh, I like this.* What luxury, to be mothered.

I worried that Georgie would accidentally hurt MK so soon after her spay surgery and so I spent all my time following them around, the pair of them, offering MK extra food and drinks of water, catnip toys and treats, distracting Georgie when MK wanted to sleep. *Georgie*, I would whisper-shout, rolling catnip balls toward her. *Don't bother your mother.* MK liked to sleep with her belly in the air and her front paws stretched straight out like a zombie, and I liked to watch her, feeling something like pride at the comfort I had created for her. Sometimes Georgie would fall asleep with her, resting her head on her mom like a pillow.

MK kept living outside my house in Poets Square, tending to the baby that wasn't hers. Monkey started warming up to both MK and Georgie; she was happy to interact with the other cats as long as she didn't have to mother them. I spent my time counting the bowls of cat food, refilling the water bowls, washing cat beds, delighting in all my daily care for all the creatures I never meant to inherit. None of us each other's mothers.

SOMEWHERE, MY MOM STILL HAS a notebook from my childhood surgeries, where she took notes on medical updates, wrote down doctors' names and medication doses, documented her worst worries and fears. She counted the number of tubes coming out of my body and wrote it down: seventeen. Her handwriting hasn't changed in thirty years.

A lot of things are passed down on the mother's side, my geneticist told me. We were talking about breast cancer, my genetic predisposition to it. But he could have meant mental illness, anxiety, poor eyesight. He could have meant the exact shade of my hair, the shape of my fingernails, the almost imperceptible cleft in my chin, like a shadow.

My face is a perfect replica of my mom's and I wonder what it's like for her to look at me. I'll never have a child with my face. I'll never have a daughter like a mirror, reflecting back the best and worst of me. Of course I think about it.

MK's face is orange and white and black, geometric, like an inkblot test. You could see anything in it.

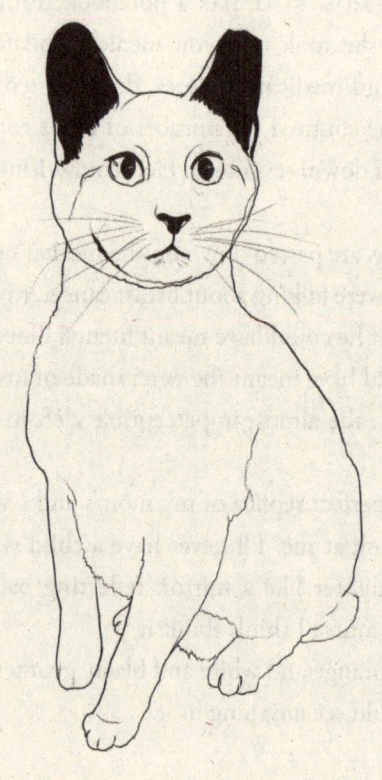

Viral Cat Videos and the American Dream

For a decade I did everything right: I went to the college that offered a full scholarship, graduated at the top of my class, got into grad school. I moved to a city with a lower cost of living, got a stable job at a nonprofit, felt like I was helping people. But it never mattered how hard I worked or how many overtime shifts I signed up for or how many hours outside of work I spent trying to figure out other ways to make money. Rent would go up again. My car would break down. I lived paycheck to paycheck. I got laid off.

There was one crucial move that saved me, one thing that catapulted me from unemployed with mounting medical debt to a homeowner with steady income and a sizable chunk of money in the bank, financially stable for the first time in my life.

Here is the secret, the thing that changed it all for me: I filmed a video about cooking a miniature Thanksgiving dinner for stray cats. And the video went viral.

I HAD BEEN CARING FOR Monkey and Georgie and François and all the other cats for over a year, and posting about them regularly on Instagram in still pictures and wordy captions. I had a small but loyal following there, a few thousand people who regularly sent donated cat food and kind messages. That was already pretty wild to me, the way people all over the world had become invested in the ragtag group of stray cats I hadn't even meant to inherit.

It was important to me that the posts I shared online weren't just sick cats and sad stories and pleas for donations. I loved the cats because they were weird, because they were strange little goblin creatures that lived their lives alongside ours, and I was always trying to capture their strange joy for Instagram.

I liked to give cats silly names and pose them for pictures: I named a kitten Party Time and crafted her a tiny party hat to wear in photos; I named a cat Mr. Business and bought him a bow tie and a cardboard laptop. I named a cat Tony Hawk and bought him a miniature skateboard, and filmed as he pawed curiously at it. *Do a kickflip*, I told him, and he purred.

People liked it, and I was convinced it mattered. Among all the sadness in the world, all the animal suffering I was seeing, all the budget spreadsheets I spent my nights studying, trying to come up with a version where the numbers didn't end up negative—I was convinced that silliness mattered.

It could have been any of those posts that blew up. Going viral was less about the actual content and more about timing, more about algorithms, hitting on some magic combination that would catapult a particular post to the top of the internet.

Occasionally I would share pictures of the cats on Reddit, and one time Sad Boy made it to the front page of the site, the first post people saw when they opened the app. He got 35,000 upvotes, and the strangeness of it—trying to conceptualize that 35,000 people liked this large feral cat who lived on my roof—left me dizzy. That night I stood in the backyard and stared up at Sad Boy where he was lounging at the end of the roof, his enormous paws dangling over the edge. I remembered the first time I saw him, right there in the same spot on the roof, looking like no one had ever loved him in his entire life.

Sad Boy, I whispered to him in the dark, *thirty-five thousand people like you. What do you think about that?*

THE IDEA FOR THE THANKSGIVING DINNER video came from boredom. Tim and I both lived far from our families and for several years we had spent all our holidays just the two of us.

That year, I saw a Cornish game hen in the store and thought how cute it was, how it looked like a miniature turkey. How shocked I would have been to know that that moment would be the start of a whole new career. Does it count as a career? Making cat videos?

I cooked my miniature turkey in a miniature baking pan. I mashed a single potato and bought a can of pumpkin puree and a pouch of turkey-flavored gravy for cats. I searched thrift stores until I found just the right plates. They had to be miniature, little saucers, and look fancy.

The plates I found were white porcelain with gold edges. The meals—a whole tray of them, one for each cat—were garnished with a single green bean each. I had obsessively researched which Thanksgiving foods were safe for cats. Tim filmed for me as I carried my miniature Thanksgiving tray outdoors, the camera pointed at my hands and the tiny plates of turkey. And then I placed the plates around the driveway, the fancy dishes on the dirt and gravel, and filmed as all the feral cats came over to sniff them. François—his face always looking confused because he was cross-eyed—was the first to take a lick.

That was the whole video: preparing miniature meals, making them look fancy, and François, with his goofy cross-eyed face, gobbling his down. *Making Thanksgiving dinner for stray cats*, I captioned it. That's all it took.

TIM ALWAYS HUMORED MY SILLY CAT ideas in a way I found charming, like he didn't quite understand what I was doing but respected it. *Just trust me*, I was always saying to him. *The internet will love this.* He would look somewhat resigned and then shake his head and say, *I know. I'm sure they will.*

Was I trying to go viral? It had never been the original intent behind the Instagram account, and even after a few thousand followers I couldn't have imagined what would eventually happen. It's true that I loved having a following. It felt like people—real people, not faceless online profiles—were invested in my work, were invested in my cats, cared enough to get updates every day.

It wasn't what I had imagined doing with my life. I had imagined being a writer—a graduate degree, a teaching job, a best-selling book before thirty—but at every stage of my career I was reminded that I was somehow already behind. The debt I took on for grad school set me back for years. The teaching jobs didn't pay enough to live. I wasn't sure how everyone else was doing it—family money, maybe, or wealthy spouses—but for me it wasn't doable.

I had never pictured myself making a living as a cat rescue influencer—didn't even know this was a job that could exist—but sometimes it was close to what I wanted to do. I had spent my life wanting to be a writer, and here was a platform, even if what I was writing was Instagram captions about cats. At least people were reading them. *This is poetry*, people would comment on my captions about Sad Boy emerging at night alongside the moon. *I love the way you write about these cats*, people would comment on a post about François, who for months I inched toward on my hands and knees, creeping closer every day with treats, until one day I finally touched him, rubbing my hand over his head, his cross-eyed face seeming to short-circuit as he realized I was safe.

Those comments, the fact that I was still writing, technically: this was enough to keep me feeling a little bit like myself.

My identity had always been tied to achievable goals for which I would be rewarded with another report card, another publication, another prize. I had no idea who I was if I wasn't a writer, and wasn't that how it was supposed to be? Hadn't we all been asked since grade school what we wanted to be when we grew up? I had worked hard for it. I had defined myself by it.

I used to imagine that by my thirties I would have my PhD, would be teaching English in an old brick building, bringing donuts to class. Writing books, wearing thick glasses, organizing my library. Now I try to figure out how to respond when people ask me what I do.

I'm a feral cat TikToker, I practice saying in the mirror, and that feels absurd.

THE THANKSGIVING VIDEO BLEW UP first on Reddit, and then on TikTok. I was using TikTok only as a tool to edit videos; I wasn't expecting to gain any followers. But then I did: ten thousand followers overnight, and then a hundred thousand by the following day. I barely knew how the platform worked—I couldn't figure out how to reply to comments at first—but within a week I was invited to join TikTok's creator fund, which paid a fraction of a cent per video view to content creators. I had made a dumb cat video on a whim and now the world was saying: *Monetize this.*

My first month on TikTok I earned over a thousand dollars. That was nearly a paycheck for me, nearly eighty hours of work at my content-writing job. Eighty hours of emails and meetings and editing and copywriting, and instead I had earned it making videos about cats. It felt so surreal and so fortunate and so likely to be a fluke—to end any minute now—that I told everyone about it, about my weird fleeting moment of internet success that would allow me to make an extra student loan payment, to have a safety net that month. Everyone I told gave me the same look, the same brief reevaluation of their own life, or of the whole system, how wrong something must have gone for this fact to be true: that making cat videos could earn more money than my master's degree ever had. Everyone said the same thing: *Man, I have chosen the wrong career.*

The next month I made over two thousand dollars from cat videos, and that monthly number kept going up. It was unclear how much TikTok's creator fund actually paid, what formula it used to convert likes and comments and shares into dollars, but for me it didn't matter. My formula was simple: the more cat videos I posted, the more money I made. For a while I aimed to post six a day—

some of them a ten-second clip of a cat eating treats and some of them three-minute stories, edited together from clips of kittens and foster cats, the full adoption stories of some of the cats from our driveway. This counted as storytelling, I was telling myself. This was something like what I wanted to do with my life.

In those first months my videos were routinely being viewed hundreds of thousands of times each, and at least once a week one would hit a million views, or two million, or ten. That would pay my phone bill for the month, or the water bill, or for a tank of gas. I was starting to pay my bills on time, and then early, and then extra, throwing money at my old grad school loans, stocking my savings account.

When I tried to learn more about what I should be doing with my money—retirement accounts, high-yield savings, Roth IRAs— I felt dumb. It only made it clearer that there were whole worlds I didn't know about, whole encyclopedias of financial knowledge, class rules, unspoken signals between the wealthy and the uber wealthy, new money and old, and I was ignorant to all of it. I was nowhere near it. The richest I'd ever been, the most money I'd seen in my entire life, and it was a couple thousand dollars from cat videos.

For so many years I had felt like I was on the precipice of poverty, one missed paycheck away from losing everything. When my videos were casually earning an extra three thousand dollars a month, I paid off old medical debt. I bought new tires for my crappy car and I went to the dentist. I was staring at numbers all the time, marveling at them, watching the safety net beneath me grow and grow.

Someone asked if I was investing my money, and I was: I was investing in more cat scratchers in silly shapes, more dollar store props for ridiculous photos. *I'm working*, I would joke, when Tim asked why I was crouched by the trash cans again, filming François as he sprinted around with a new toy. The cats were so exquisitely filmable, the way Georgie liked to sleep in a pile of leaves and Mr. Business lounged with his gray-white belly up and François kept getting startled by his own tail, jumping a little, pawing at it.

It was absurd to look out my window at a group of feral cats and know that they controlled my financial future. François would roll over in his little driveway bed and accidentally fall out, his goofy face looking all around like he didn't understand how he had ended up on the ground, and I would be cursing myself for not getting it on camera.

I HAD NEVER FELT MUCH SHAME about not having money, mostly because I didn't know how much more of it some people had. I was mostly able to pay rent on time, and I had health insurance, and those things combined seemed to be more than most people had. Everyone I knew was also young and broke, drowning in debt, getting all their furniture free from the side of the road. I was resourceful. I was surviving in a system that was hard to survive in.

I had grown up in an old Massachusetts mill town, a depressed little working-class city. My ideas of money, of what counted as rich—they couldn't begin to account for the kind of wealth I would someday see. Eventually, picking up cat food donations from the nicest neighborhoods in Tucson, I'd see houses in the foothills with big double-ended driveways and four-car garages, impeccable landscaping, fancy gates that cost more than a year of my rent. I had seen wealth on TV and on social media but I hadn't understood it as a real thing; I hadn't realized how many people were living lives I couldn't understand. I hadn't even realized people had car payments;

I had always driven the same decades-old Camry that had cost a thousand dollars cash.

I don't know how I hadn't noticed it before—maybe I was tuning it out on purpose; maybe it didn't seem relevant—but people all around me were showing off money in ways I didn't even know how to read. It was a code I had never learned, signs that were completely foreign to me. Tim had friends from a wealthy family, and the first time I met them all I could think about was how nice their teeth were. My retainer had broken years earlier and I couldn't afford to replace it, and each morning I frowned in the mirror to see the dark gaps between my teeth growing wider.

———

I STARTED SELLING T-SHIRTS. I hadn't thought there was any real demand for branded merch; I had nearly a million followers then, but I figured that a person who casually enjoys watching cat videos is not necessarily a person who wants to spend money on a T-shirt featuring a cat from the internet. But people kept asking. A local artist designed shirts with François and Sad Boy and Lola and Monkey, all the cats I filmed all day in my driveway, and we sold them as pre-orders so we could print the exact number of shirts that sold. I figured we'd sell a few dozen.

We got over a thousand orders. That first round of merch—a few silly shirts of the cats as cartoon characters, a tote bag, some stickers—netted me an easy ten thousand dollars. I barely did anything: I approved the designs and I shared them on TikTok, and within a month the money was in my bank account, a solid round number, all those zeros.

What do I do with this? I asked Tim.

He stared at me. *What do you mean?*

There had to be a catch.

I opened a new savings account, one that would pay me interest on every dollar I saved, and after that I watched each month as my money turned into more money. That was it. There was no catch.

———

EIGHT MONTHS AFTER THE THANKSGIVING VIDEO, I got laid off from my job. My real job, in a real office, where I got a steady paycheck for writing fundraising content for the food bank. I cried when I had the conversation with HR, some leftover panic from the life I had been living a year before, where a single missed shift could have left me without meals for the week. I was still living in that mode, still carrying that stress, even though for eight months I had been living comfortably because I had cooked a Cornish game hen for cats. I couldn't stop thinking about it, how different it would have been just eight months before. How quickly would I have gotten another job? Who could I have asked for money? Tim's paycheck alone couldn't have covered our expenses for long. I imagined the long spiral of events, all the bills I would've fallen behind on, all the things I could have tried to sell to catch up. Sometimes I still looked around the house at everything we owned, inventorying everything worth any amount of money, in case I ever got desperate again.

But I had money. The cat money, we called it. I got severance from the layoff, too. My bank account felt so full it might burst, a feeling I had never known before. Officially, I was unemployed. I couldn't call myself a writer. Most of my videos by then were of the kittens I was rescuing throughout the city, the stray cats I was trapping to spay and neuter. Now I was suddenly free during the workday, and I spent my days saving more cats. Making videos about them.

WHEN PEOPLE ASKED WHAT I DID for work, I would sometimes say I was a cat rescuer. Sometimes I would keep it broader—*I work in animal welfare*, I would say—although this didn't feel particularly true when my to-do list for a day was often things like "Buy a miniature couch for a kitten" and "Get footage of François for TikTok." People would assume I worked for a shelter, cleaning kennels all day, when actually I was recording voice-overs from my couch and responding to comments on Instagram.

A lot of the time I *was* rescuing cats—I was climbing through trash, crouching in parking lots, spending hours at a time trying to catch an injured cat so I could rush it to the vet, so I could stay up all night in the waiting room sobbing, waiting for updates. But I wasn't getting paid for any of that; it wasn't my job. *I'm an independent cat rescuer*, I tried saying, so people wouldn't think I worked for our local Humane Society or county shelter, but then instead people would ask, *So then how do you make money?*

I had a deep fear that someone would think I wasn't a cat rescuer but just a rich person cosplaying as one. I wanted to prove how hard I was working. I wanted to tell everyone online: *I promise I'm counting every penny in my bank account. I've never been more aware of exactly what I'm worth.*

I was worried people would think I was independently wealthy, or living off Tim's salary so I could spend my time making dumb videos for the internet. I don't know what I thought I had to prove—so what if I *was* sitting home on the internet all day, filming feral cats out the window? But it felt inauthentic to let people believe I wasn't working hard for what I had. Maybe I was worried people would assume I was lazy. Maybe I had felt so much shame about not having money that now I felt shame about having it.

I was happy—and more financially stable than I had ever thought possible—but there was still a nagging part of me that couldn't reconcile my actual life with the one I had imagined. I had built my worth around advanced degrees and prestigious awards, traditional career milestones, and now I had a TikTok account and a yard full of cats.

I still wanted to tell people I was a writer. Sometimes I thought about how to bend the truth, how to give myself a job title that made me sound more like myself. What I really wanted was to avoid calling myself an influencer, and I definitely didn't want to be called a TikToker. I started saying *content creator* and then changed it to *social media storyteller*.

My job was always in flux, constantly changing, and also was not really a job in any traditional sense. I was making money from my content, but the heart of what I did had nothing to do with editing videos. It was a weird dual job: I had to do the work of rescuing cats and also the work of turning rescuing cats into consumable, monetizable content. I couldn't afford the rescuing without the content and couldn't create the content without the rescuing.

Tim was always meeting new people and they were always asking what I did for work and I was worried about what he would tell them. *What do you tell people when they ask what I do?* I asked him, and he shrugged like he genuinely didn't know. He said: *I just say you do . . . cats? Her job is cats.*

TO THE CATS, THE MONEY meant nothing. They didn't know anything about having a job, or about how much more soundly I had been sleeping since knowing I could always pay the rent. Before I was laid off I would sometimes go outside before work and sit in the driveway with the cats, watching François play clumsily with his own tail, and think enviously: *He doesn't even know what email is.*

But the cats—all cats—were existing under capitalism alongside me. They were as affected by money as I was: all those early days when I hadn't been able to buy them cat food, all the months I waited until they got vet care. It was easy to ignore the effects of money when I thought of them as animals. They didn't have jobs or bank accounts or generational wealth; they couldn't understand that all the new beds I bought them came from selling their own faces on T-shirts. It was easier to think about when I remembered that I was an animal, too, living under systems that often felt rigged against me.

How often I wished I could explain to the cats that if they could do something extra cute on camera, I could buy them more treats that month, or that if I wasn't home that night it was because there were other cats to help. *Not all cats are rich and famous like you*, I would tell François, touching my finger to his very pink nose and watching him get confused by it. Remembering how skinny he had been all the first months I knew him.

Money determines everything: whether cats get basic vet care, whether they have steady meals, whether they'll live indoors and sleep in soft beds or reproduce in dark alleys, searching dumpsters for scraps. There are pet cats and there are stray cats and sometimes they feel like two distinct social classes of the same species.

I'm convinced the wealth gap between them is growing.

There are cats with their own social media accounts who go for walks on leashes and in little pet strollers, who have a closet full of little cat clothes, who eat a raw organic diet. There are cats whose people pay out-of-pocket for cat chemotherapy, for black market medications to fight rare cat diseases, anything to keep the cat alive for another year. And everywhere, all over the city, in backyards and parking lots, there are cats dying. There are cats scrounging for food and cats giving birth and cats who will never sleep in a bed or see a vet.

Tim liked to pitch video ideas to me, most of them purposefully absurd. *What if you took out all the money you got this month from TikTok*, he said, *and scattered it around in small bills?*

I started to answer but he held his finger up like he wasn't done. *And then*, he said, *have François roll around in it.*

———

ONE OF THE COMMUNITY CAT PROGRAMS I started volunteering with keeps a map of the city, little cat-shaped pins dropped at every address where there are large numbers of cats living outdoors. The patterns are obvious: the clusters of pins are very clearly in the poorer neighborhoods. The south side is covered in pins, covered in cats, the dots of the map overlapping each other. The west-side neighborhoods that are mostly mobile home parks. The east side, past the US Air Force base, where there are no low-cost vet clinics.

On the north side, in the foothills, where the homes cost a million dollars and are built right into the mountains: there are no stray cats there.

A year after the Thanksgiving video I was delivering donated cat food to twenty-three different addresses every month, people who were doing their best to help stray cats but couldn't afford it. I drove a lot of cats around, too: picking up stray kittens on the south side and delivering them to fosters in the foothills; pulling cats from high-risk shelters along the border and driving them to rescues in wealthier areas. My car was new. When my old one finally died I had been able to afford a new one, an SUV, chosen because it could comfortably transport at least ten cats in traps. My life had changed drastically in material ways in under a year, and it was because of cats, because of the internet, because of a video I had edited on a whim. It was so arbitrary, all of it, even the fact that I had inherited the cats at all. The more I thought about the cats, the more I thought about money. The more I thought about money, the more I thought about cats.

Before the cats, I thought about money constantly but not always consciously. I would wake up from dreams where I had missed a payment on old medical bills and the hospital had agreed to cut me back open and take my organs as collateral. I thought about money as finite and bad, as abstract, as numbers that funneled into my account biweekly and then funneled right back out, diverted to a thousand bills. Money was numbers in a column and there was never enough of it.

But once I had money, I only thought about it more. Was it possible to have this much money? Could I lose it all? Had it changed me, on some fundamental level? At the same time that my weird internet success had allowed me to catch up on bills, I was witnessing poverty that I had never known: the neighborhoods where I was trapping cats, the houses that bore the signs of generation after generation getting poorer and poorer. All the years I had called myself broke I hadn't known how much worse it could be. I became anxious about money in a way I never had been. I finally had money and I could lose it all at any moment.

I didn't want to spend my time watching my number of followers fluctuate. I didn't want to always have a camera in my hand. Sometimes a video would perform poorly and I would get a pit in my stomach. That was it: my moment was over, and I had made as much money as I could, and now I had the rest of my life to figure out what was left of my career. How I would ever apply for jobs again with the gap in my resume that just said *cat influencer*. How long I could make the money last. I started having dreams about François being kidnapped and held for ransom, his confused little face looking out at me from somewhere dark. I didn't have enough money to buy him back. I had spent it all already.

I spent half my time convincing myself that I deserved it, that what was happening to me was everything I had ever worked for.

I spent the other half of my time marveling at how it could have happened to anyone, how if it hadn't been me—at that exact moment in the algorithm, in that exact house full of cats—then everything would still be the same: my underpaying job, my mounting debt, my ancient car struggling to start each morning.

My daily life—my every morning with the cats in my driveway—started to require a constant reconciling of this. That I had done it: the American dream. That I just as easily could have been—almost was, and still could be—a victim of it.

It wasn't impostor syndrome that had me constantly questioning my worth. It was a genuine question, an understanding that under capitalism any of us only succeeds because others don't. Was this true of cats? I started eyeing François like he was a member of the ruling class. All my success, my happiness, my stability, my cats: it was all an anomaly. Every day, every bill I paid, I was thinking: *Do I deserve this? Do I deserve this? Do I deserve this?*

In This One the Cats Don't Survive

When Dr. Big Butt died I didn't believe it. I had already written his story in my head—he was friendly, and I would find him a home, and when he died someday it would be of old age, at the end of a happy indoor life of catnip and warm beds and treats—and then instead his story was over, just like that. I couldn't reconcile it in my brain. I truly didn't believe he was dead, to such an extreme that I worried about my grasp on reality.

That can be a normal manifestation of grief, my therapist told me. The word *grief* didn't sound real. He was a big orange cat. He was gone.

But he's not gone, my brain said.

It was a year after we had moved into the house, and six months since the colony of cats had stabilized; they were all fixed by then, and already many of the friendlier cats had found homes. The remaining cats—Dr. Big Butt among them—were healthy. They had put on weight. We had all settled into a routine, the initial shock of suddenly having thirty cats having worn off, and it finally felt like after all the chaos I had done it. We were stable. I had saved them.

We had lost cats already, that first year. Stephanie, a sweet fluffy black cat, had been hit by a car and instantly killed. Three white kittens had been eaten by coyotes. There were other cats—BeeBee, Rihanna, TimCat—who simply disappeared and never showed up again, and I told myself stories about them ending up somewhere in a loving home, after having been seen and scooped up by someone. I didn't want to imagine the alternative.

I hadn't known how to grieve any of those losses. It hadn't felt like I was allowed to. There was too much loss too quickly and too many cats still to save, and all my energy had gone into moving on from those deaths and trying to prevent the next one. That first year I carried a deep undercurrent of cat sadness with me, but there was no time to process it, no chance to frame sweet memorial pawprints or think about what I could have done differently. When Stephanie died, I allowed myself exactly five minutes to cry. I set a timer. At four minutes and fifty-nine seconds I stopped the timer before the alarm went off. I wiped my eyes. I got back to it.

But we were past all of that. All those sick cats we started with, all the skinny cats and crusty cats and injured cats: Dr. Big Butt wasn't one of them. He had always been healthy and enormous, even when we first found him. He was a giant orange cat with a giant orange head and he liked to ram his face into me, headbutting me with as much force as he could. He loved catnip and crunchy treats and sitting with me in the front yard. His nose was as pink as an eraser. I never worried about him.

SOMETIMES MY JOB IS SAVING KITTENS, or trapping feral cats for routine vet care that I know will save their lives. Sometimes it's delivering cat food, feeding cats who haven't eaten in days, and then watching them lick their little paws after a meal. Sometimes I get to see a cat I saved living safely indoors now, or a whole colony of cats I trapped now thriving, or a kitten I rescued growing up. Sometimes there are happy endings.

Sometimes it's much bleaker. When a cat is hit by a car, when a cat is grievously injured, when a cat is ancient and weak and can't go on and their instinct is to find a hole somewhere and stay there for weeks as they die slowly, as they suffer, cold and alone and unloved—my job is to trap those cats, too. Sometimes my job is to lure cats toward me so that I can bring them to a vet where they'll die.

In my more dramatic moments, I feel like an executioner. It doesn't matter what my rational brain says. It doesn't matter that all the internet comments say: *You're saving them from suffering.*

I know.

You're giving them a gentle end.

I know I am. I know I am, and it still feels just as bad.

Often, I wake up as early as I can stand it and I start my daily cat tasks—the laundry, the scrubbing, the scooping—before the day gets too hot. All the morning vet appointments, all the empty carriers in my car that need to be cleaned. By noon I am hot and exhausted, questioning why I do anything, falling asleep on myself. I sleep fitfully through the afternoon, wake up feeling heavy, pack the car to drive out at dusk, when all the cats are coming out. When all the suffering starts again.

Sometimes I wonder if it's how search-and-rescue dogs feel, when they're trained to look for life but all the bodies they find are already dead. Sometimes I feel like my job is to drive daily around the city and search for signs of suffering and then just stand there, failing to do anything about it. *This can't be good for me*, I think. I am so often sad to my core.

DR. BIG BUTT WAS a deep orange. His eyes were yellow. I feel like I have to tell you every detail about him, like if I can't perfectly reconstruct him I have failed. I have failed him once already.

Later, I would find myself getting angry with people who didn't understand how orange he had been. People would say that they, too, had an orange cat, but they would show me a picture and their cat would be pale, light orange, like a creamsicle. Dr. Big Butt was *orange*, nearly red, this gorgeous auburn cat, the color of pumpkin pie. It was almost like it was their fault—the people who couldn't understand his orangeness—that I couldn't save him, like if they had really appreciated the richness of his color he could have survived. I wanted to shake people to make them understand.

Dr. Big Butt had a gentle calmness about him, a serene lion of a cat. His fur was always warm from the sun. His name came from an episode of the show *Bob's Burgers*. Tim and I heard it in those first weeks at the new house, when we knew there were a lot of cats outside but hadn't named them all. *What a great name*, we said. *We should name one of the cats Dr. Big Butt.*

I remember the exact spot we were sitting in the driveway—farther down, by the road—petting the cats. We had seen a big orange cat from a distance, but he hadn't let us near yet. The sun was just setting. The orange cat walked toward us, his paws padding silently along the sidewalk, his slow lumbering gait. The sunset lit him orange and pink and he looked radiant, walking toward us, and Tim and I said it at the exact same moment: *That's Dr. Big Butt.*

FOR ALL THAT CAT RESCUE WORK has given me—a community, a sense of rootedness, a purpose outside myself—it has also given me an intimate knowledge of suffering, a witnessing I never meant to inherit.

When it wasn't acute heartbreak it was the constant undercurrent of suffering. I had known theoretically that animals suffered but now I had seen it. I had seen it in my own driveway, all the times I watched exhausted starving cats trying to get to the last of the food when I couldn't afford more. I had seen it all over the city, as I got involved in helping cats in other neighborhoods. I had seen it all, and every time I thought I had seen it all I would see something worse, cats dying from things I hadn't imagined yet, cats barely alive, sights I would have nightmares about for months.

I had witnessed the staggering scope of pain and death and neglect, and once I had seen it, I couldn't take a break from it without feeling guilty, without knowing that at any moment I wasn't helping cats, they were suffering without me. It was like grief but more nebulous than that, grief for every animal that had ever existed, grief for things that hadn't even happened yet but that I couldn't prevent. It was like watching the movie *Bambi* over and over, but only the moment when his mom dies, the pure wretched animal grief of it, and then climbing inside that emotion and living in it.

AT THE ANIMAL HOSPITAL the emergency vet saw Dr. Big Butt's name and gave him a little salute. *I see he's a fellow doctor*, he said, and it was silly, but it made me feel like they took him seriously, like they would treat him well. A fellow doctor. I have never forgotten it.

Dr. Big Butt was a grateful animal, the kind of cat who seemed to understand when people were trying to help him. One of the first things donated to the cats by an Instagram follower was a little padded mat. It wasn't even a bed, just a small soft surface, sherpa and fleece. When I laid it in our driveway Dr. Big Butt was the first to come over. It was too small for him, but he didn't care; he stood with all four paws squeezed onto the little square and he purred and arched his back, stretched his legs, curled himself into the tightest circle he could, his orange fur overflowing. For weeks he was always on that mat, rolling over on it, flexing his paws, looking blissful.

Watching Dr. Big Butt on that cheap mat, that tiny piece of fleece, I realized that he probably had never felt a soft surface before in his life. Before that he had slept every day on pavement or curled in the dirt. That first time he stepped onto the mat he blinked like he couldn't believe it, that anything could be so soft, that anyone could be so kind. Giving a stray cat his first soft bed: I couldn't name the feeling I got, but I knew nothing else would ever compare to it, knew I would do whatever I could to feel it again, knew it would be worth any amount of grief.

———

I'VE SPENT NIGHTS AT EVERY animal hospital in town. I've spent nights with cats I love, sobbing, begging them to live. I've spent nights with cats I'd never met before, cats I know nothing about except that they're dying, and that I found them, and that if I can't save them, I at least won't let them go alone.

I've trapped cats dying slowly of cancer, cats starving to death because of tumors in their mouth, cats attacked by dogs and left for dead. Cats with urinary blockages and bad kidneys, cats who have inexplicably become allergic to their own teeth. Cats who are frozen or overheated, panting, rigid.

You would not believe it, how vast and how varied the suffering can be. It's my job to understand how bad things can get, to face the reality of animal suffering, like the burden of a clairvoyant who can predict tragedies but not prevent them. Your pet cat curled softly in her bed: I know everything that could ever happen to her.

All the nights at the emergency vet, it's never just the animals—the gory injuries, the emergency surgeries, the pets who don't make it—but the people. The sobbing couple who walks in with a dog and leaves with just a leash. The tags on the collar still jingling.

I THOUGHT I REMEMBERED IT perfectly, that morning I saw Dr. Big Butt and knew something was wrong. I thought I remembered it all: the emergency vet, the overnight stay, all the vet bills I approved, the money a friend loaned me, the begging I did at the front desk, telling them to approve any cost, just do it, just do whatever they needed to do. I thought I remembered the phone call. The feel of his fur in my arms.

Maybe grief has dulled my memory. Maybe I've tried to forget.

It was still dark out, five thirty in the morning, when I went outside and saw him. Dr. Big Butt, big and orange, blinking in the brightness of the carport light I had just turned on. He was climbing out of one of the cat cubes I had gotten him, and he was fine. His head was fine; his front half was fine. He was coming to see me, pulling himself out of bed to nuzzle his head into mine. That was the moment—that seconds-before-disaster moment, suspended in time—that I would think about later. The last moment before I knew. He climbed halfway out of the cube, large and perfect and orange, and then I saw it: the back half of his body wasn't working.

It was some kind of embolism, I would learn later. A clot. Something in his veins that had paralyzed him instantly, destroyed the back half of his body. Later, I would make the mistake of googling it. *Incredibly painful for the cat*, Google told me. *Always fatal.*

The vet worked to stabilize him for a full twenty-four hours. It didn't matter. The next afternoon a friend drove me back to the vet. What a terrible ride, knowing what we were driving toward. There were no other options. He was suffering.

I held him, heavy and orange, and kissed his giant forehead. I went home and sobbed until I threw up.

GRIEF FOR ME FEELS EXACTLY like nausea, like a deep aching inside my joints. When I turned thirty I was diagnosed with arthritis, and when the doctor asked me to describe the pain I told him it felt exactly like sadness, the deep gnawing of it, the constant grinding hurt.

The most well-intentioned of my friends listen to my stories—the sick cats I've stayed up all night to trap, the cats who were already dead when I found them—and say things like: *I could never do it.* I don't know how to explain that I can't do it either. People are always saying how hard it must be, but there is no special hardness about me.

Without meaning to, I have removed myself almost entirely from the reality of what I experience. I can completely detach myself from the things I've seen. I learned to do it after Dr. Big Butt died: how to split myself in two, how to shield my brain, how to get through another night at the vet without forming any memories along the way. You could read a list to me of all the dead cats I've known—every single one I couldn't save—and it would feel to me like hearing about someone else's life. *That's a lot of cats to lose*, I would think. *That must be so hard.*

I've seen things I hope I never see again. I know I'll see things even worse. *I don't know how you do it*, people tell me, and I want to say: *Me neither.* I weep exactly as much as you would.

———

SOMETIMES WE WOULD CALL Dr. Big Butt DBB for short. Or The Butt. Tim was always up before me in the mornings and sometimes he would wake me up with a cat report. *The Butt's outside*, he would say softly, kissing my forehead, and I would get out of bed just to see him, just to take my tea to the driveway and wait for a big orange cat to lumber over and flop down at my feet.

When I got home from the vet with my empty carrier, without Dr. Big Butt inside it, I climbed into bed. It was midday. I had no plans to ever get out of bed again; I couldn't think of anything to do with myself but to rot, heavy and sad, sweating into my sheets. The idea of getting up, of moving my body, of ever even looking at another cat again: it was impossible.

It would be years before I recognized it as a pattern. After every loss, every overwhelm, I would crawl back into bed. Once, a feral cat had fallen into a bucket of motor oil and escaped coated in it, slowly dying, his body unable to regulate the summer heat through the oil slick, his pancreas failing as he licked more and more oil off himself. I spent night after night crouched in the alley where he lived, waiting for him, trying to catch him. I was tracking the oily pawprints he left through the dirt. I never caught him. I never found him dead.

The woman who fed him texted me after we tried for weeks. *He doesn't show up for food anymore*, she wrote. *The pawprints have stopped.*

I had stalked the alley with a net, I had set every trap I owned, I had climbed over neighboring walls trying to find him. I was delusional without sleep, exhausted. Every moment of his suffering was my fault.

I sobbed on the couch with my head in Tim's lap. *I want to get in bed and never get up again*, I told him.

I know, he said. *You say that every time.*

That didn't feel true. Each loss felt uniquely unsurvivable, like I had never been through it before.

Really? I asked him. *And then what do I do?*

You get in bed, he said. *And then eventually you get up again.*

———

A YEAR AFTER DR. BIG BUTT died, the very same day, I was at the same emergency vet with another dying orange cat. I hadn't meant to notice that it was the day he died; I had not purposely made note of the anniversary. My phone reminded me. My phone sent me a notification that said *Your memories from this day last year: pet friends!* and the memories were all photos, Dr. Big Butt's face, swaddled in a blanket in his final moments.

That day I was driving to another cat colony, one with dozens of cats, where I had started trapping five at a time for vet care. Those cats didn't have anyone feeding them, no one looking out for them, and so I was on a rotating schedule with a few other volunteers, each of us taking turns driving over to put out big bowls of food, to refill the water bowls, to do a quick survey of how many cats were out each day, how many more we still had to help. That day it was my turn.

I knew most of the cats there, but that day—that dumb anniversary day, my phone buzzing to remind me of my own dead cat—there was a new one. Orange. He was matted and moving slowly, something off about him, and I was quickly assessing how sick he was, wondering if I could trap him then or afford to wait until the next day, and then he turned his head and I saw it: a deep sickening wound, a gash across his whole neck, festering and necrotic. I want to say I felt something about it, that I felt sick to my stomach at the sight. I didn't. I had seen it before, with so many cats, so many times. I felt only exhaustion, only a sick, ragged grief.

The cat walked right into the trap. He died at the vet's office. He was big and orange and I couldn't save him.

———

LATER, I WOULD LOSE an orange cat named Karl Havoc. I would lose Jurgen, the gentle black cat who showed up in the driveway one day and then never left. I would lose cats that had seemed immortal, cats I hadn't thought it was possible to lose. The sadness got easier—they were older cats, and their time had come, and they had passed peacefully in my arms, and surely I should be used to it by now—but it also compounded, each sadness another brick in a great wall I was building in my brain.

I would try to save cats named Lichen and Lobsterfest and Blueberry and Disco, and every one of them is dead now. I would try to save cats who died before I even got a chance to name them.

I've spent a lot of my life cautioning myself against redemptive narratives. The idea that bad things happen for a reason, that traumatic things can be made meaningful because we grow from them: it never appealed to me. I spent much of my childhood sick and much of my young adulthood struggling, and none of it made me a better person. It drove me crazy, the way people would try to assign my misfortune a purpose. *Sometimes bad things are just bad*, I was always telling my friends. I would have screamed it from the rooftops if I could have.

I want to say that when I found that other orange cat a year later, I saved him. I want to say it made me feel better, every orange cat I saved in Dr. Big Butt's memory. I especially want to say that it's worth it, all of it, that when I get in bed, I know that I'll get up again. But that's not the point. The point is that every time I crawl into bed, I am admitting defeat, am consumed by it, am certain that this is the time it won't be worth getting up again.

He knew love, people kept telling me, like it should make me less sad.

You were there for him in his final moments, people say, like that didn't make it worse. Like I could ever forget his gasping agonal breaths.

I never wanted to tell the story of losing Dr. Big Butt as if it had a happy ending, like he had died but inspired me to save so many other cats. His death in my mind remains stark and unyielding, meaningless, not made better by any cats that came after him. He died and I kept helping cats despite it. He died and he shouldn't have.

I thought about making a bumper sticker: *My cat died and it didn't make me a better person!*

My cat died and all I got was this bitter resentment. My cat died and all I got was this deep gnawing sadness.

———

AFTER DR. BIG BUTT WAS GONE, I kept seeing him in the driveway. It wasn't insane. He had been a cat and there were still dozens of other cats around. Every paw, every tail, every sign of movement: I thought it was him.

What I had left of him was a single whisker and a print of his perfect pink nose. For weeks I found his orange fur around the yard. For months I wondered if there were signs from him I was missing. Surely he would send me some new orange kitten to save, an orange butterfly landing on my hand, a single orange leaf falling on my rainy windshield while I cried in my car. I felt stupid for wanting this, my dumb brain desperate to make meaning from grief. At night I sat on a rock in our front yard where Dr. Big Butt used to crawl into my lap, pushing his big orange head hard against my hand, and I cried until my eyes were swollen, cried until the tears gathered at my chin. I looked at the sky and I tried to feel his presence.

It's been years now. I have been asking him to haunt me.

———

I FEAR I'VE MADE Dr. Big Butt more orange in my memory than he was in real life. I picture him so rust-colored and enormous, unlike any other cat that has ever lived. I rarely revisit pictures of him—they make me cry—and he has grown so vast in my mind, so massive in my understanding of grief and despair and getting out of bed again, that he has taken on magnificent proportions, colors that cats don't even come in. In photos he is a regular orange cat. In my memory he's still walking toward me at sunset.

It has been so hard to feel good about a world where hope feels like a stupid thing to have. I've held all my hope in the tiny bodies of cats, the cats I've saved, the cats I've seen transform, the cats who are alive through small acts of care by people trying hard. I've wrapped my entire worldview in it—cats, how much it matters when we take a moment to care for them, how content they look on the first soft surface they've ever felt—and when they die it shatters me. It sends me to bed. There's no version of myself that could ever be enough to save every one from all suffering and it haunts me, it destroys me, it keeps me up at night.

I don't want my main emotion to be despair.

I've been trying to identify it, the feeling that guides me.

Sometimes I think the feeling is smallness, all the good and bad of it. How small I feel in the face of all of it: the suffering, the vast numbers of cats that need help, the impossibility of saving them all. How small I feel among the cats, like I'm the same size as them. How small the moment was, that first time Dr. Big Butt padded across the driveway on his big orange paws and leaned his body against mine and closed his eyes, like he was transferring something holy into me. How that has kept me going.

Trash

I got a call about an injured kitten.

The caller said that the kitten was skinny enough that they could see his spine. I never knew what to expect when responding to these kinds of calls. People would say *kitten* to describe anything from an hours-old newborn to a one-year-old cat, and *injured* to mean anything from having a small scratch to literally already dead.

I never even knew where I was driving: I would plug in an address and let my phone lead me there, my car packed with traps and carriers and tuna and towels, water and gloves and kitten formula. I never knew if I was driving to an apartment complex or a business or a landfill or a house, or who would be waiting for me there, or how it would go. At some point my repeated exposure to these kinds of situations had erased whatever social anxiety I had once had. There was no point in feeling anxious: there was a cat who needed help, and there was me, and whatever other circumstances existed would be condensed to nothing as I closed the space between us.

The kitten was at an apartment complex on the east side of the city. The man who had called met me in the parking lot. *I can't find it now*, he said, and he was crouching under a white pickup, peering up into the engine. *I think he was in there when I turned the truck on.*

The apartment complex was called Desert Palms, and it was abandoned. Or it looked abandoned: the windows were boarded up, the dumpsters overflowing, the chain-link fence around it graffitied and cut open, with human-size holes where the wires had been wrenched apart. There were tents set up in the alley, mattresses piled by the dumpster, broken glass all over the ground. The building itself didn't seem habitable.

My job was to think like a cat.

I had done this enough that I knew exactly where to look. I searched under the cars in the parking lot, inside the dumpster, in the dark spaces under the dumpster where it rested on pallets. Inside each trashed mattress that had been chewed open to reveal its springs. There was a long row of dense bushes at the back of the parking lot. Another fence, all these cat-size holes tunneled underneath it. Trash everywhere. I searched.

What I found was a bunch of other cats. Ten of them, at first, but then I saw more and more—sleeping in the shade of those bushes, scattering from under each car in the parking lot. There was trash all over the ground and someone had added cat food among it, and the cats were picking at it, pawing at each piece, trying to find the kibble among the fast-food wrappers and Styrofoam cups and cigarette butts. Across the street there was a house with a falling-down fence and trash piled in the yard and everywhere: more cats. We hadn't found the kitten. I was getting the sinking feeling I got almost every time I responded to a call for help. The feeling said: *There's a much bigger problem here.*

The man who had called about the kitten seemed embarrassed to be living there. He was staying with his mom, just for a little while.

We try to keep to ourselves, he kept saying when I asked about the other people around, about who might be feeding the cats or know more about the kitten.

The people here—he started, and then seemed to reconsider. *I don't know. It's just a trashy place. We're trying to get out of here.*

I watched the other cats for a while. It was the height of summer, 115 degrees.

The apartments here don't have running water, the man said, almost like an apology, and I realized that the parts of the building I had thought were abandoned had people living in them. It looked like each unit had once had an air conditioner but most of them had since been stolen, leaving rectangular holes in the walls. I watched a cockroach scuttle out from one. The cats were scavenging around the dumpster, and I was watching the broken glass under their paws. We did not find the kitten.

———

AT HOME THAT NIGHT I googled Desert Palms. The complex had been recently bought by a property management company a few states over. On their website, the pictures didn't show the boarded-up windows or the broken-down cars. The website described it as a gated community. You could click a button right there on the website and instantly pay a $2,500 deposit to rent an apartment, without ever having seen the building in person.

I went back a few times that month with no plan other than to look at the cats, to assess the situation. There were at least fifty cats between that parking lot and the yard across the street. There were syringes in the bushes, a lot of foot traffic in the dark. Sometimes someone living there—either in the apartments or the tents outside them—would approach me and I would tense up, feeling unwelcome and afraid.

It was true that the apartments didn't have running water. Two tenants were suing the property owners. Another was trying to sue the city. Half of the units were vacant, although often they weren't the units you'd guess. The apartments with no locks on the doors and plywood nailed haphazardly across the only window: there were people living in those. Were they paying rent to live there? Were they squatting? I didn't ask.

The city had done a recent round of evictions, and everyone who had been forced out was now living in their cars along the street. Everyone I met there told me this—*Those cars and tents are all the people from the empty apartments*—but somehow I didn't believe it until I met Peggy, a woman in her seventies who walked hunched over a walker. She lived in a white car with a smashed windshield. She asked me once if I could bring her a gallon of water, and another time if I could help her find a bucket she could use as a toilet.

My job was cats—that was what I knew how to do—but most of the cats there were in better shape than the people. Usually when I worked on a feral colony, I could trap all the cats, get them to the vet, and help pay for cat food for whoever was feeding them. And that would be it: another job done. But at Desert Palms—I didn't know where to start.

On TikTok, I was always giving each new cat colony a public name so I could refer back to them. The names I gave colonies were silly: there was the Big Cheddar Colony, where all the cats were named after cheeses; the Storm Colony, where we named the cats things like Windsock and Cold Front and Downpour Mike; the

Diet Coke Colony, where a single kitten had wandered out from a shed and sat next to a can of Diet Coke the exact same size as him.

In our rescue group chats we called them the Desert Palms cats, but online I didn't want to reveal the actual location. None of the cats had names yet. There was only one defining thing about the cats at Desert Palms: the huge amounts of trash piled among the bushes and scattered across the parking lot, the piles of garbage that the cats lived among. It became their name: the Trash Colony. The cats—the identical trio of black cats, the crusty kittens, the little calico, the dozens of orange tabbies—became our Trash Pals.

Most of the cats at Desert Palms seemed to be coming from the house across the street. It's hard to describe it as a house. The building had clearly burned at one point, had suffered catastrophically from a fire and had been condemned by the city. The bright orange notice from the fire department was still on the plywood boarding up the front door: *NO OCCUPANCY.*

A makeshift fence of mismatched boards and bungee cords made it impossible to get onto the property, but I could peer through the slats. The yard was full of cats. I counted ten cats, twenty cats, thirty cats. It was full of trash, too. One corner of the yard was just a pile of beer cans, old tires, unidentifiable plastic. Rusty metal. Big charred piles of wood. Trash. This is where the cats were coming from.

There was someone living there despite the warnings on the door. The neighbors told us about him: Richard. They told us: *His house burned down but he's got nowhere else to go.*

When I met Richard he immediately threatened to kill me. By that point I had perfected my pitch: I knew exactly how to walk up to a total stranger and suggest that they let me catch each one of their cats to get them spayed or neutered. I knew how to get the information I needed—*Are there cats inside the house, too? Are they healthy? Are there kittens? How many cats total? Do any of the cats need critical vet care?*—somehow without conveying judgment, without scaring people away. I had spent most of my life practicing social skills in a mirror and suddenly it was useful, the way I could put on a persona: I could stand in the middle of fifty starving cats and have a casual conversation with their caretaker, make it seem like everything was fine, like I wasn't ready to retch at the smell. I could persuade anyone to let me start with just a few cats—*Let's just get these two spayed, just a quick checkup from the vet, and go from there*—and end up with all fifty at the vet.

But it didn't work on Richard. He would kill me if he ever saw me in the neighborhood again, he said. He didn't need anyone messing with his cats. I had left my phone number on a note on his fence, and in his texts that night he sounded unhinged, writing in all caps and run-on sentences.

CATS ARE FINE, he wrote. *DO NOT COME BACK HERE. DO NOT WANT TROUBLE BUT DO NOT WANT HELP.*

For a month I would show up at the Trash Colony a few times a week to put out food and water for the cats. It was easiest if I went early in the morning; the neighborhood felt safer in daylight, and Richard was usually still asleep.

I started picking up trash there out of necessity: there was so much of it that I couldn't find a flat surface to put out a bowl of water. I would rake through the trash with my hands, pushing piles of it into the small trash bags I had started keeping in my car. The cats were living in a long row of oleander bushes and the bushes were growing in more trash than soil.

Some of the trash was drug paraphernalia but a lot of it was evidence of all the other ways people were trying to survive: fast-food wrappers, water bottles, toothbrushes, empty bottles of Tylenol. Empty alcohol bottles and batteries, old flashlights and stray socks, all sorts of unidentifiable wet and crusty things.

Sometimes people dumped bigger things—tires, cardboard boxes, old office chairs—and sometimes the cats would claim these things as beds. Once, I arrived with my cat food and my trash bags and found that someone had dumped a pile of framed paintings and the cats were sleeping on top of the art. I took a picture of it and for a while it was my phone background: a black cat I had named Dumptruck sleeping on a painted seascape in a tarnished brass frame. All the trash around him.

Picking up trash there was practical but also strategic. Technically I didn't have permission to be on the property, and although so far no one but Richard had cared, I didn't want to cause problems. Most complaints about feeding feral cats are about the messes they make, and it seemed like basic public relations to not contribute to the mess there. Who could say the cats were causing problems if the property seemed to have a little less trash day by day?

It was also an olive branch, an effort at helping the people who lived at Desert Palms in whatever tiny, tangible way I could. Each time I arrived to check on the cats I met someone else who told me about the squalor inside the apartments, how unsafe the area was, how often the cops were around. *They're charging me nine hundred dollars' rent to live here*, a woman named Crystal told me, *and every night the man who used to live here tries to break back in through the window.*

It was uncomfortable to show up with my car full of cat food and fresh water and tend to the cats—I had started bringing treats, too, and catnip—and offer nothing to the human residents. I was aware of my discomfort, and trying to interrogate it—*Why is it easier to help animals than people? What does it say about me? What am I perpetuating?*—but I also didn't know what I could do about it. I couldn't bring breakfast every day for everyone who lived at Desert Palms. I couldn't pay their rent. I didn't know how to turn their water back on or get them air conditioners. Once, Peggy dragged her walker up to me, limping more severely than usual, and showed me an open, rotting wound on her foot. *I think I can take a bus to the hospital*, she told me, *but I can't pay the hospital bills once I'm there.*

I stared at her foot.

I have no idea how to help, I said, and I hoped she could tell from my face how desperately I meant it.

But I could pick up trash, and I did. I filled trash bags from the row of bushes where the cats lived, and from the parking lot, and from the row of apartment doors. I picked up empty bags of chips and cigarette butts and beer cans, and I picked up condom wrappers and dental flossers and bits of rubber tubing and burnt spoons. I picked up the bowls after the cats ate. A man named Howard was always outside his apartment, shirtless and smoking. I had been picking up trash for a month when he acknowledged me, nodding his head almost begrudgingly toward my trash bag. He said: *I've been seeing you.*

RICHARD'S THREATS TO KILL ME were a roadblock. I kept showing up to check on the cats and feed them and make sure they had water, but each time I reassured Richard that I wouldn't trap any of them. I wouldn't take them away. It's horrible practice to feed stray cats without getting them fixed; it went against everything I worked for. *Why not just call animal control on him?* a fellow rescuer suggested. *What if you called the police?*

I didn't have a plan. Richard continued to send long, often drunken texts accusing me of stealing his cats, even on days when I hadn't been near Desert Palms. A man named Cliff was living in his car outside Richard's house, and one afternoon he asked if I had any dog food, if I could help him with a hot meal.

I stayed and talked with Cliff for a while, his dog crunching kibble at our feet. Cliff, with a mouth full of french fries, chewed and nodded toward me. *What organization are you with? Like, why do you do this?*

Oh, I said. *No organization. Just a person.*

You know Richard? Cliff said.

I nodded. *He wants to kill me.*

Cliff nodded back at me. *I'll tell him. I'll tell him you're all right.*

———

AFTER THAT I BROUGHT DOG FOOD every time I fed the cats at Desert Palms. Sometimes I brought breakfast for Cliff. Howard had started waving a friendly greeting every time I visited. Peggy had asked if I could help her get some blankets before the weather cooled, and I did.

It was a month after I had first discovered the cats there—a month after Richard's first threats to kill me—that I got a phone call, a scrambled voicemail, the voice on the other end urgent.

> Courtney. It's Richard, um, with the cats. Listen, I'm in the hospital, I've been here for four days, I don't know when I'll get out. No one is feeding the cats. There are cats inside my

house. Kittens. I'm not there to feed them. I don't know who to call but I'm worried about my cats. I guess I'm just wondering if you can help me feed the cats until I get out. I'm sorry for calling. I don't know who to call. I'm sorry.

I drove over that night and Cliff helped me unhook all the bungee cords on Richard's gate, and we wrenched down boards until we could get in. The cats were streaming out of the house. I started filling bowls with food and the cats ran toward them, descended upon them in clusters. I cleaned the water bowls, left huge amounts of food for the cats too shy to approach while I was there. I picked up trash.

I fed Richard's cats every day for two weeks while he got his foot amputated. He was diabetic. It came out of nowhere, he said, the gangrene on his toes.

It would have been the perfect time to start catching the cats, to get them fixed and bring them back. Would Richard notice? Would he care? I had explained to him many times that I wouldn't keep any of his cats—they would come right back to him but a little healthier—but he hadn't believed me.

One little calico was always the first to greet me when I arrived each night to break into Richard's property, and each night I resisted the urge to scoop her up. The cats would follow me across the street when I refilled the food bowls at Desert Palms, and I would have to chase them back to the sidewalk as cars sped by. There was constant foot traffic in the neighborhood, a lot of fights, too many people struggling to survive. At least once a night the cops would cruise by and there was a collective holding of breath, everyone living on the streets trying for a moment to seem invisible. I was always thinking about Richard's early text to me: *DO NOT WANT TROUBLE BUT DO NOT WANT HELP.*

Just please, Richard said every day on the phone from the hospital. *Don't take my cats. They're the only thing I've got.*

WHEN RICHARD WAS RELEASED FROM the hospital, the first thing he did was count all his cats. *I'M HOME,* he texted me. Always in all caps. *I COUNTED THE CATS AND THEY'RE ALL STILL HERE.*

I told you I wouldn't take them, I texted back.

THEY ARE HAPPY TO SEE ME, he wrote.

I'm sure they missed you, I told him. *I'm glad you're home.*

There were always long pauses between Richard's texts, sometimes hours, and I knew he was drinking. I had surreptitiously cleaned up a bunch of beer cans from his yard while he was hospitalized, trying to pick up just enough that he wouldn't notice I had helped.

I decided to push my luck. I texted Richard again: *Would you let me spay just a few of the cats? I promise I'll bring them back.*

He responded right away: *I GUESS THAT WOULD BE OKAY.*

I recruited my friend Gerald to help with the cats at Desert Palms, and when he trapped the first cat there we named it after him: Feral Gerald.

It was hard to keep track of the cats—there were so many and they all looked so much alike—but we named each of them: Dumptruck, Dinky, Crusty, Tropicana, Mr. Trash. Turnip and Kevin and Pulp-Free Orange Juice. There was one we just called The Fluffy One and one we just called Tiny Calico. We trapped them all, one at a time, and drove them to the vet. They came back, one at a time, spayed or neutered, vaccinated, healthy. Richard oversaw our work, alternating between gratitude and anxiety and anger. It took months doing it this way, and as Richard got more comfortable, he started texting me more and more often, later and later at night, clearly drunker and drunker on the other end of the phone.

THIS IS A PICTURE FROM WHEN I WAS SIXTEEN, he texted once, and it was: there was young Richard, unmistakable, surrounded by people who must have been his family. *I AM THE ONLY ONE LEFT FROM THAT PICTURE WHO IS STILL ALIVE.*

Another time Richard confessed that he had been in trouble with our county's animal control years before. He never figured out who reported him. *THEY TOOK ALL MY CATS*, he texted. It was two in the morning and I wouldn't see his texts until the next day. *TWO YEARS AGO I WAS IN THE HOSPITAL AND THEY TOOK EVERY ONE OF MY CATS. I CALLED AND CALLED BUT I NEVER SAW THE CATS AGAIN. I DO NOT KNOW IF THEY KILLED THEM ALL.*

Past a certain level of drunkenness Richard's texts would switch to lowercase, to succinct sentences. *you know ive been thinking*, he texted once, after we had trapped and returned all fifty of the cats that lived between his yard and Desert Palms. *since i don't have any family left ive been thinking that these cats are kind of like my family.*

———

THE FANCY FEAST I KEPT in my car to feed the trash cats was all donated, sent to me from my Amazon wishlist from people all over the world. My followers on Instagram had fallen in love with the cats at Desert Palms just as I had: they had seen Dumptruck and Mr. Trash rummaging for food near the dumpster, Crusty waiting in a dumped cardboard box for a meal. Whatever we needed for those cats—new water bowls, more treats, cans of tuna to entice them into traps—people bought. When I added dog food to the wishlist for Cliff's dog, someone donated it instantly. *No dog should go hungry!* the gift note read.

I started adding other things to the wishlist: blankets, bottles of water, hand warmers, and first-aid supplies. Trash bags. I wanted to share supplies with the people at Desert Palms, too, and I wrote a long Instagram caption about all the need we were seeing in the neighborhood, about how it wasn't only the cats that were suffering. It was something of a bellwether, when I saw this many cats struggling to survive: it almost always meant that people were struggling to survive, too.

By then my followers had shown that they could donate thousands of pounds of cat food overnight, could stock an animal shelter with months' worth of supplies, could raise thousands of dollars for a cat who needed vet care. But the items I had added to the list for people—winter hats, wool socks, protein bars, and soup—didn't move. No one donated them.

Why was it so much easier to feel compassion for the cats? I spent a lot of time watching Dumptruck, who had grown sleek and shiny after months of good meals, as he played in the bushes. He walked with his butt high in the air, like his back legs were a little too long. The cats were innocent, uncomplicated in their needs. They hadn't made any bad choices that had led them to this parking lot life. It was easier to feel that people deserved the harm in their lives. What had Dumptruck done to deserve this? What had Dumptruck ever done wrong?

THE NIGHTS WE SPENT TRAPPING cats at the Trash Colony had become something like block parties. It was a strange dynamic, the way the neighbors had started to welcome us, and it felt like we had invented a new way to bring a neighborhood together. The stray cats living among the trash: a reason for all of us to organize.

It so often felt bleak there, at Desert Palms. The nights were getting colder and the people living in tents would light fires to stay warm, and sometimes the fires would spread down the alley until sirens would sound in the distance. Every time I drove up I never knew what I would find: a cat newly injured, a new pile of trash near the cats' food bowls, neighbors we had gotten to know newly evicted and living on the street. Peggy had had a stroke and was in the hospital, and someone stole everything she owned from her car. Someone had left a loose dog in the parking lot and suddenly we were feeding him, too. Richard went back into the hospital and then came home again, over and over in an endless cycle, and he knew he no longer had to ask. We would be there at his gate every day to feed the cats.

There was a constant police presence in the neighborhood, the cats lit by flashing blue and red. There were overdoses. There were weapons brandished. When Gerald came with me he came armed, and sometimes when we heard voices rising from the alley I could see him instinctively put his hand to his hip, ready to defend. I couldn't imagine a situation in which the gun would do anything but make things worse. I carried Narcan and cat food.

On the nights we spent trapping cats outside those apartments, we ordered pizzas and hot breadsticks and spread the boxes on the hood of Gerald's car. We brought sodas. It wasn't something we had originally planned, the cat-trapping picnics. It was just that we were showing up to this neighborhood that wasn't ours, this place full of so much human need and human survival, and by then the cats were getting better care than the people. The cats were getting free vet trips, looking increasingly healthy and sleek, sleeping in warm little shelters we had built them for the winter. The people—more of them every day, forced into homelessness—were struggling. We were hitting record low temperatures that winter.

Cliff had asked to learn how our cat traps worked, and he helped us fill little bowls with tuna. Richard would sit outside his gate like he was watching a parade, shouting out to us as each cat passed by. *There's the other black one! Here comes a kitten! This is the mom, the fluffy gray one! The one you still need to trap!* We'd share pizza with anyone who walked by, and hand out blankets and hand warmers and bottles of water. We must have met the whole neighborhood by then: Terrance and Larry and Rob, Peggy and Crystal and Deb. Howard had started helping us pick up trash. Someone would always offer alcohol and we would politely decline—we had to drive vehicles full of cats back to the clinic after—until we didn't, and then it would be a Friday night in the dark at Desert Palms, all of us sipping drinks and watching stray cats play in the trash.

IT WAS A SIX-MONTH PROJECT, getting all fifty of those cats fixed. It took building relationships in genuine and incremental ways. At some point it stopped being about the cats there; I worried about Dumptruck and Crusty and Feral Gerald, but I worried more about Peggy, about Cliff, about Howard. I was constantly checking the police scanner for activity near Desert Palms, and when there was a shooting or a stabbing or an overdose I would call Richard, check in with Terrance, drive over to check on everyone there who didn't have a phone.

We could have fixed all the cats faster if we had just done it. Technically we never needed Richard's permission to trap the cats; we could have trapped them across the street so we weren't on his property. We could have trapped every one of the cats those first weeks Richard was in the hospital, and if he hated us when he got home then so what? His cats would be fixed and we could just never go over there again, block his number, hope for the best. I could have turned the whole neighborhood over to animal control the second Richard threatened to kill me, and for a while—getting run-on texts from Richard at two in the morning, thinking about all the cats still reproducing in his yard—I wondered if I should have. I could have called the police. Would they do anything? Could I get a police escort to catch stray cats in a rough neighborhood?

I never had a plan, but I knew it couldn't involve animal control, couldn't involve the cops, couldn't be based on any kind of fear or retribution or punishment. I was always thinking about Richard's early texts, about the time all of his cats were taken away. It was a punitive model of animal welfare, an approach that managed to penalize both people and animals for what often amounted to a lack of resources, a lack of trust. Richard had lost his whole family, and after that he only had cats, and then someone took them all away. It was no wonder, when he saw my dumb eager face peering through the slats in his fence, offering to help, that he had said no.

Sometimes, now, Richard still texts me and Gerald in the middle of the night. Sometimes his texts are about the cats or about his childhood or about whatever is new in the neighborhood, but often they are a single sentence, the same sentence, every time: *I love you both as friends.*

WE REACHED A TURNING POINT in the trash pickup: we were finally cleaning up trash faster than new trash was appearing. The ground around the cat bowls was clear. We could see the soil under the bushes. Sometimes I could tell that someone else had been helping: I would get there and see that a whole section of the bushes had been cleaned up, raked out, and a new water bowl had appeared there instead. Sometimes cat toys would appear. One day I pulled up and saw something in the bushes—another piece of old furniture dumped, and now I would have to figure out how to dispose of it—only to realize that it was a brand-new cat tower, a beautiful carpeted cat tree with high perches and dangling toys. Dumptruck was tucked inside of it, sound asleep.

Nearly a year after I got that first call about the injured kitten, I pulled up to Desert Palms and found police cars parked along the street, six or seven of them, lights flashing. All the tents in the alley were gone. The white car where Peggy lived had been towed; Cliff's black van was gone. All the blankets we had brought them, all the supplies: they were in the dumpster like trash. Howard was outside, staring silently at the scene.

I didn't know what to do so I followed my normal routine: I scattered treats for the cats, and as they ate I put on gloves and shook open a trash bag. The police lights were reflecting off everything. The cops were deep in conversation with an older woman I didn't recognize, and I eyed the interaction as I picked up trash. There was less and less of it, the trash, and I only had half a trash bag filled when the cops finally approached me. They asked what I was doing.

My friends live here, I told them. *I'm a volunteer. I feed the cats.* I held up my trash bag, my gloves still on. The cats had scattered.

Okay, one officer said.

I didn't know how to phrase my question. I gestured vaguely toward the alley, toward Richard's house. *Where is everyone?*

Oh, yeah, the officer said. *We're just cleaning up the area.*

I was still holding a dirty soda bottle I had picked up from the bushes.

Just making it safer around here, the other officer said, and the kindness with which he said it to me, like I'd understand, made the implication clear: I was someone who deserved safety, and everyone they had just displaced—poorer people, homeless people, people of color, people using drugs—were a threat to it. It was never my neighborhood—I didn't live there—and now I was the one still there, unbothered by the police in the parking lot while I fed stray cats, while the original residents had been evicted and then criminalized for trying to survive on the streets. Peggy, Larry, Cliff. I could see another officer peering over Richard's fence, noting the orange sign on the door. Richard was legally not allowed to live there.

Just cleaning up the neighborhood, I could hear an officer saying to someone else, like it was an official mandate he was forced to recite, and my gloves were covered in mud. My bag still half full of trash.

Letting Myself Go

We were on the second floor of a hospital parking garage. I was on the ground. It was filthy all around me—all the grease and oil baked into the pavement, the cigarette butts littering the cement floor, the can of cat food I had opened and then abandoned, its beef-flavored gravy spilling down the sides. There were faint meows coming from somewhere inside the undercarriage of a car, the high pitch of kitten cries, and I was shimmying my way under to search.

The car was a Mercedes. I didn't know anything about cars, but I understood just from looking at it—just from how low to the ground it was—that it was expensive. Its driver was a doctor, a thoracic surgeon just off a twelve-hour shift. The woman who had called me about the meowing was a nurse. It was seven p.m., shift change, and all around us there were nurses and social workers and radiology techs, surgeons and phlebotomists and physicians. They were all in scrubs or pressed chinos, their hair slicked back, their jewelry sparkling. From under the car, I could mostly see their feet passing, all the loafers and Hokas and clogs, all the colors of scrubs on their legs.

The thoracic surgeon needed to get home. He couldn't wait there forever. It was common for kittens to end up in car engines, and when I had gotten the call thirty minutes earlier, I already had everything I needed in my car: a cat trap, a cat carrier, my bite-proof gloves. My brightest flashlights and my long-handled kitten grabber—an extendable pole with a soft pinching grip on one end, just the right size for extracting kittens from hard-to-reach places. I hadn't bothered changing clothes, and the pants I was wearing were my last good pair, the jeans with the fewest cat food stains.

The kitten wasn't in the engine. He was somewhere in the back half of the car, somewhere between the rear wheels, and I couldn't find him. The thoracic surgeon was pacing. I had begged him to give me ten more minutes, and then ten more, and ten more. Every time I spoke to the kitten he would meow back to me, his cries getting raspier and more panicked, more urgent, and I couldn't let the surgeon drive away with a kitten trapped under his car. The car was too expensive to aimlessly wrench around on, but I didn't know what else to do. The nurse who had called me had enormous eyes and she was crouched next to the car, her hands clasped together in worry, looking to me for guidance. *What do we do?* she kept asking.

We jacked the car up. We unscrewed the heat shield. The kitten cried and cried from somewhere I couldn't see, and I was trying to imagine him, what color he might be. How old. *I hear you, buddy*, I kept saying. *I'm trying to find you.* The surgeon was sitting in the front seat then, rubbing his keys between his fingers like he might start the car at any time. The nurse was wide-eyed, flitting around, opening more cat food. I was running from one side of the car to the other, listening to the meows, trying to triangulate the sounds to figure out exactly where they were coming from. I was throwing myself on the ground, crawling under the car, getting up, running to the other side, and throwing myself back down. I didn't notice how gross any of it was, how dirty my hands were turning.

After an hour—the thoracic surgeon having given up and gotten on the ground with us—we saw him: a little gray baby. His little gray tail. He was trapped on the rear axle of the car, balancing, his body almost black with exhaust. It took another ten minutes to get my hands up there, to get a good grasp on him, and while I did it I didn't think about a single other thing. The bottom of the car was only an inch above my face and the kitten was staring out at me, nervously licking his lips, and it was just me and him and I had exactly one minute left to get him to safety.

When the kitten—we named him Benz—was safely in a carrier, I stood up and brushed my hair from my face. Staff were still filtering into the hospital, all the matching scrub sets and Crocs, the hospital IDs on colorful lanyards, the perfect ponytails and close-cut shaves. I was wiping sweat from my forehead. I was shaking with adrenaline. The thoracic surgeon drove away. The kitten was safe.

I had never felt so accomplished, so heroic, in my life.

When I got home, I glanced in a mirror.

Oh my god, I thought. *This is what all the hospital staff saw standing in their parking garage.*

My hands were black from reaching up into the car to wrestle the kitten out, and where I had wiped my face there were long swipes of grease and exhaust across my nose and forehead. The grime was collecting at my ears and neck. My hair was sticking up at weird angles and when I tried to brush it out the brush wouldn't budge; when I had lain on the ground and turned my head I had rubbed all the oil and grease into my hair, and now it was clumpy and stiff. My bright yellow shoes were bloodstained, one from an injured kitten I had picked up weeks before and the other with my own blood from a bad cat bite. I had stopped shaving my legs. My ankles were covered in long, scabby scratches from a patch of thorny bushes I had pushed through the night before, when I was trying to set cat traps as close as I could to an abandoned property I couldn't access. My pants had new cat food stains. My shirt had a picture of my own cats on it.

Oh, I thought, considering myself in the mirror. What was shocking wasn't that I looked filthy or insane. What was shocking was that I hadn't even thought about it. That night—crawling around a parking garage in a panicked attempt to save a kitten before a doctor drove away—felt like the first time since childhood that I had done anything at all without thinking the entire time about how I looked.

FOR MOST OF MY LIFE I've been picking myself apart on a microscopic level. At age ten I got a magnified mirror for my birthday and I became obsessed with it, how I could see every pore on my face. Every eyebrow hair. Every crease. I spent too much time looking at my teeth up close, and for my next birthday I asked for Crest Whitestrips. By age fourteen I was underweight but worried I was fat; by sixteen I was skipping meals and running endless laps. I wouldn't leave the house without spending a full hour with my hair straightener, smoothing down my side bangs again and again. I wouldn't leave the house in the rain.

When friends had pool parties, I wouldn't swim. When friends had lunch, I wouldn't eat. The only place to hang out in my hometown was the bowling alley, and I hated it, how bowling required me to get up in front of everyone and turn around, how everyone would be watching.

There was nothing especially unique or extreme about any of it. I was like every teenage girl in an image-obsessed world, every girl who grew up with magazine covers pointing out our imperfections. The danger for me wasn't just the anxiety or the self-obsession, the hours I spent staring at myself from every angle, the mirror I kept in my middle school backpack to double-check my hair. The danger was the way I felt when I got it right. The validation when I looked good and got compliments, the sweet victory of it.

I was eleven the first time I learned a boy had a crush on me. His name was Christopher, and he was in my fifth-grade reading class, and something about it—that a boy could look at me and see something he liked, something he wanted, that he might even think about me when we weren't together, that maybe he lay awake in bed at night and thought about me the way I thought about so many of my classmates—made me feel better than I could ever remember feeling.

I already lived for validation. I worked hard in school so my teachers would like me, did all my chores at home so my parents would like me, made friendship bracelets so my friends would keep liking me. But something about a crush, even a middle school one, opened a new world for me; it was a kind of validation I hadn't known existed. A whole untapped spring of ways I could seek approval, ways I could feel a fleeting sense of accomplishment, a hot flushing reminder that I existed.

That a person—a boy, a man—could look at me and think: *Wow, she looks great.*

I shivered to think of it. At eleven I already knew somewhere deep inside me that for the next decade I would chase that feeling.

———

WHEN I FIRST STARTED the Instagram account for the cats, I kept it anonymous. It was less a decision and more the default option; it was an account about cats, not me, and it was more interesting to share photos of feral cats than photos of my face. For a while I didn't include any information about myself at all—my name, my age, my gender—and as I gained followers, I would sometimes get comments that said things like: *I'm so curious about the person running this account!*

I always responded the same way. *I'm actually not a person*, I would say. *I'm just a pile of cats in a trench coat.*

For most of my life I lived like I had cameras on me at all times, an invisible array of people I had to look good for even when I was alone. I curated my invented audience, imagined it was my mom or my teachers or the person I had a crush on, or some vague idea of a person, maybe a man I'd meet someday and need to impress, constantly imagining how I'd be perceived. It was exhausting.

Did I really never do anything that took my full attention? Did I really save one part of my brain, reserve a portion of my daily energy to at all times remember to keep my stomach sucked in, my jaw set in the right position, my hair tucked the right way behind my ears?

It was my job—and I understood this from age nine—to perform. To perform cuteness as a kid, prettiness as a tween, sexiness starting somewhere around age fourteen. To perform was to be perceived, constantly, by men whose motives I didn't understand. The first time I was catcalled I was twelve. By twenty-two I thought it was a great superpower of mine, my looks. My ability to understand what men wanted, the way I could contort myself to fit the exact shape of whatever kind of woman they wanted in their lives.

Being in my driveway in the dark with thirty cats around me, sharing faceless stories online: that was the first time in my life I didn't feel perceived. I wouldn't realize it for years, the experiment I had unwittingly set up for myself. It was the first time since childhood that I received attention and praise for something that I could be certain was wholly unrelated to my looks. In high school I received academic awards and classmates half joked that it was because the teachers had crushes on me. In college I told professors I got into a PhD program and one of them told me I also had nice legs. Like these were the same: my intellect, my ambition, the shape of my legs. Whatever I achieved, whatever anyone said, I could never be sure I had earned it. I could never be sure it wasn't tied to the body I inhabited, the beauty I tried hard to perform.

Online, sharing cat stories, no one knew what I looked like. I took pictures of the cats the same way I took pictures of myself: over and over again, trying every angle, every source of light, scrolling through hundreds of nearly identical photos until I found the one that looked best.

WHEN I HEARD MEOWS FROM inside a dumpster I climbed inside, all the way in, with all the rotting food and trash. When I couldn't get to a sick cat on the other side of a barbed-wire fence I climbed over it, tore my arms up, ripped my pants to shreds. The summers in Tucson stretched on, 110-degree heat every day, and even the simplest cat rescue—just standing in the shade with a can of tuna—

would leave me drenched in sweat, my face red, my hair frizzing up into sweaty curls. I was often meeting new people who already knew who I was—*I follow your cats on Instagram*, people would say, smiling, like they were meeting a celebrity—and I'd realize later that the first time they met me I was inside a trash can or under a house, covered in spiderwebs, red-faced and sweating. *I don't usually look like this*, I always wanted to say.

Sometimes that was true. For a while I tried to keep my different lives distinct: there was my cat life, where I was always sweaty and wearing stained clothes and crouched somewhere weird, and there was the rest of my life, where I still styled my hair, still cared about what I was wearing. I still spent time staring in the mirror, cataloging the new lines appearing by my eyes; I still flitted anxiously about before going to work or to dinner or to see friends, as if anyone cared how straight I had managed to get my hair. I still thought about it, much of the time: how I looked, how I came across to other people, what a total stranger might think of me.

But the boundary between my lives was porous. Increasingly I would trap a cat and drop him off at the vet and then run a few more errands before driving home; often I would stop somewhere for a late-night snack after trapping cats all evening. I was showing up at the grocery store looking wilder and wilder. More and more I found myself in public with my hair completely undone, my face bare, my clothes dirty and mismatched; I found myself in public as versions of myself I had spent my whole life trying to disguise. As saving cats occupied more of my time, I started giving up everything that felt superfluous: straightening my hair, shaping my eyebrows, shaving my legs. The image of myself I kept in my head, my precise and abiding understanding of how other people saw me: it got blurry.

It had felt like an accomplishment, for most of my life, to be in complete control of how I looked. To have an exact image of myself in my head and to know how to manipulate it. Which meant that the more cats I saved, the more I got involved in the community, the more I spent my energy on anything other than myself, the more I felt like I had failed at something. I couldn't even picture myself anymore. In my mind I was still twenty-two and perfect. In photos I looked middle-aged and surrounded by cats.

At some point I started to wonder if I *was* just a pile of cats in a trench coat. It was somehow easier to picture—a pile of whiskers and fur stacked on top of itself, formed into the vague shape of a person—than myself, my actual human form, which I seemed not to recognize anymore. It was jarring to realize that my appearance had changed and I had barely noticed it. When had my hair gotten so frizzy? When had I gained ten pounds? When was the last time I shaved my legs? I texted my friends, all of us women in our thirties grappling with a lifetime of being made to understand that our appearance—our youth, our beauty, our appeal to men—was the most valuable thing about us. That we were steadily declining commodities, that we should be clinging to our beauty as it left us like a receding tide. I texted: *I've really been letting myself go.*

BEFORE I EVER FOUND the cats in our driveway, before Tim, I occasionally rescued dogs. I didn't mean to; my office was in a neighborhood where dogs were always getting loose, and eventually I started keeping a leash and a bag of Pup-Peroni in my car just in case. A few times I volunteered to walk dogs at the shelter or sit at work with a stray dog until someone could pick her up. I always made sure to get pictures, any time I was helping dogs. I wanted to look cute, smiling in a photo next to a shelter dog. I wanted to look selfless and impressive. I wanted to use the photos for Tinder.

That was how I did everything, how I conceptualized my entire existence: as performance. As something other people were watching, something other people were judging, something I could document and trade in for feelings of validation.

I filtered everything in my life through the lens of male attention. That was what mattered; that was how I constructed my entire self-worth. All my value as a person, all my merit: it was all tied up in how men felt about me, how attractive they found me, whether they would swipe right or left on me when my face popped up on dating apps. It didn't matter if the attention faltered, if a man left my life. Male validation was in infinite supply. I could always find more.

I wouldn't have admitted it. I'm not sure I even understood it, how much attention from men buttressed my whole identity, my entire idea of myself. It wasn't that I didn't value all the other parts of me, all my talents and accomplishments. It was that they weren't the same without an audience, without male approval. When I graduated college at the top of my class, volunteered, saved dogs, ran half-marathons, got into a PhD program—all of that only mattered to me if someone was watching. If I looked good to them.

FOR A WHILE I TRIED specifically not to collect cat shirts. It seemed like the last bastion of sanity to me, of caring at all how I looked to strangers. In my twenties I had cared so much about how I presented myself at work each day that I downloaded an app to track my outfits; I took pictures of every item of clothing I owned and the app cataloged them in a virtual closet, and every night in bed I dragged the little pictures around my phone screen to assemble outfits, mixing and matching trousers and blouses and blazers. Now I was trying hard to remember that version of myself.

The cat shirts snuck into my wardrobe anyway, as they were always bound to do. Sometimes shelters I volunteered for would give me one of their shirts for free. Sometimes my friends and family would give me cat shirts as gifts; I had been hard to buy for and then suddenly I wasn't, because everyone knew exactly one thing about me: cats.

The cat shirts were goofy and dumb, with cartoon cats and silly slogans. I wore them. They got ruined quickly from army-crawling through alleys to catch feral kittens, or tossed out because I had held a cat with ringworm close to my chest and the shirt wasn't worth disinfecting. At first, I only wore them for cat-related things—trapping, vet trips, transporting cats from one shelter to another—and sometimes to bed.

And then suddenly I was traveling, waiting in the Denver airport for a delayed flight, when I realized what I was wearing. The airport, where once I would have pictured every man I might meet along the way, the way they might look at me, the person who might have the seat next to me on a flight, how they would perceive me, how they would rate me on a scale of one to ten. Once I would have worn something conspicuously uncomfortable, my cutest shoes, my most padded bra. It was never clear to me who I was trying to impress, or why. Only that I had to; it was my imperative as a woman to look good, even in the airport, even when I had been up since the night before for a four a.m. flight. And then one day, three years since the cats appeared in my driveway, I was at the airport and I looked down at myself like I didn't remember getting dressed and found that I was wearing jeans that didn't fit and a shirt that said *CAT MILF.*

I wore shirts with cats in cowboy hats saying *Meowdy*, cats on surfboards, cats dancing under a full moon. I wore shirts with pictures of my own cats, drawings of my own cats, silly slogans about my own cats. Vintage cat shirts, bootleg cat shirts, shirts where the front showed a lineup of cats and the back showed their rears, their tails raised, their little cat buttholes. *Is that what you're wearing?* Tim would ask, when we were getting ready to get dinner with his friends, and I would look down at my own shirt and realize it was covered in buttholes.

FOR ALL THE TIME I spent on TikTok making cat videos, I also spent time scrolling the TikTok FYP—the For You Page, a never-ending feed of videos chosen by an algorithm just for me. Sometimes the algorithm made wild assumptions about the kind of content I wanted to consume. Sometimes it was clear that the only thing TikTok knew about me for sure was that I was a woman.

Every day I would get videos about antiaging routines. Videos about hair products, hair wash methods, makeup products, skincare, teeth-whitening, eyebrow microblading, manicures. How to analyze my face shape, how to analyze my body type, how to know if lip filler was right for me. A hairbrush that would make my hair shinier. A serum that could take years off my face. A serum for sun damage, a serum for skin brightening, a serum to make my pores invisible. I should be dermaplaning and ice-rolling. TikTok videos taught me the names of all the lines forming on my face: crow's-feet, smile lines, nasolabial folds. The lines between the eyes are called elevens. *There's a product for that*, TikTok told me, and I watched videos of women younger than me stretching long pieces of tape across their foreheads before bed.

All of it—the obsessive skincare, the ten-step hair routines, the names for bodily flaws I hadn't known existed—was branded as self-care. Things I should be doing for myself. Things I was failing at.

It all felt true to me—there was still a twenty-year-old inside me who understood the world through obsession and control, through male validation and the ability to mold myself to fit the exact shape of it—and it also felt false to me: horribly false, malevolently false, at best a way to keep women spending money and at worst a way to keep us distracted and pliant, too busy staring at our pores to notice anything else in the world.

Sometimes I asked Tim: *Do you ever wish I didn't have this specific line near my eyebrow? Do you ever wish my skin was more hydrated and dewy? Would I be prettier if my lips were one milliliter larger in volume?*

What? he would say. *No.*

I was influenced, too, by the increasing number of comments on my videos wondering what I looked like. I could chalk most of it up to curiosity—some people had been following my cats and my rescue stories for several years by then and had no mental image of me, didn't even know my name—but some were more insistent, more specific, like they were trying to goad me into proving them wrong. *If she hasn't shown her face yet it's probably because she's ugly lol*, one comment said. I looked at myself in the mirror. *Maybe*, I wanted to respond. I looked up the price of the wrinkle tape that promised to change my life.

The minutiae of things I was supposed to fix about myself, the things I was supposed to perfect—it seemed like it had gotten worse since I was a teenager. I couldn't have kept up with it if I wanted to;

I was glad not to try. Was I letting myself go if I didn't commit to a seven-step skincare routine? Was I giving up on myself if my pants no longer fit? Who was I failing if I let myself go?

If I didn't curl my eyelashes, if I used the same crusty mascara I had had for two years, if I stopped wearing makeup at all. TikTok kept showing me videos about a serum that would make my eyelashes grow longer. As a teenager I used to pluck my eyelashes out one by one to calm myself down after panic attacks. What relief, to realize now that I never think about my eyelashes at all. What peace in my mind.

How long does your evening skincare routine take? TikTok videos asked. *How I do my makeup in under thirty minutes. Full hair wash routine in under two hours!* Time itself had started to mean something different to me: how many hours it took to trap a cat, how long the drive to the county shelter. How late I could stay up to still spend thirty minutes in my driveway in the dark. If I would still have time for all my cat food deliveries if I showered the next morning. I wondered sometimes how much time and money I had spent on my own looks since childhood, how much of my brain had been used up on my lifetime performance of beauty. What it cost me.

THE KITTEN FROM THE HOSPITAL parking garage—Benz—was uninjured. He got a bath, a good meal, a heating pad in a soft bed. In his little shelter kennel he liked to roll over with his belly in the air, asking for belly rubs. His belly was so small it only took one finger to rub it.

Do you recognize me, buddy? I asked him when I visited before he got adopted. I was a different version of myself then than I had been when I pulled him from the car; I was wearing clean pants and clean shoes, my hair freshly blow-dried, my eyebrows filled in. Sometimes I felt like I was letting myself go and sometimes I felt like I was pulling myself back together, creating a sturdier version of myself. I was realizing that there were several versions of myself and that they could all exist at once.

I had begun to value my moments with cats not only as escapes from myself—chances to forget completely that I existed in a physical form—but as ways to inhabit a truer sense of myself, a version of myself where I looked however I looked and it didn't matter. The cats didn't care. Rubbing my index finger along Benz's soft belly, the size of a kiwi, his hearty purr echoing. His tiny gray nose, his little animal noises.

It was the cats—the cats in my driveway, the cats I've trapped in neighborhoods all over the city, the cats I've saved and the cats I've failed to save—that prevented me from having an identity crisis as I reached my thirties and felt less attractive. *Who cares*, I find myself thinking, looking in the mirror at how my eyebrows have grown uneven. There are little animals out there; there are people depending on me. There is suffering and pain, there is care and affection, there are bright thriving spots of hope in the world. There are soft small kittens purring under my thumb. And I'm supposed to care about how I look? I'm supposed to trace the wrinkle forming between my eyes and feel like I've failed?

The Hotdog Man

The Hotdog Man always came after dark. He must have: every night the cats would tuck themselves into tree branches and roof crevices and the wheel wells of cars, hungry and waiting, and every morning we'd find them feasting on slimy chunks of hotdogs that had been scattered across the ground.

This was a new group of cats, a colony discovered by a woman named Taylor who had moved into an apartment on the west side of town and then looked outside after dark and couldn't believe what she was seeing, the dozens of pairs of glowing eyes peering back at her from the little courtyard. She was twenty-two, just out of college, starting her first year as a teacher. She told all her friends about it, how she had moved into a new place and it seemed to come with thirty cats.

Wait, one of her friends said. *Do you follow that lady on Instagram? With the thirty cats?*

That's how I ended up at Taylor's building, watching the cats climb her fence and jump to her roof, sneak out from under her car, shimmy under the fence to the property next door and then sprint away into the dark. I always did some reconnaissance before starting work at a new site like this. I liked to go right before dusk so I could see things in daylight—holes under fences, the little places where cats traveled, the hot spots. I looked for bowls, beds, kibble on the ground. Signs that someone cared, clues to who I should be trying to connect with. And then as darkness fell, I would see the cats themselves, all of them emerging at once, all over the property.

Yeah, I told Taylor. *You definitely have thirty cats.*

I had brought big water bowls and cat food for Taylor, and as we looked around for good places to set things up—unobtrusive, where she wouldn't get in trouble for feeding the cats—I kept seeing sandy shriveled bits of meat on the ground. *What's going on here?* I asked Taylor. *What do I keep seeing?*

Oh yeah, she said. *Those are the hotdogs.*

I learned about the Hotdog Man long before I ever met him, piecing together bits of his story from Taylor's neighbors like hearing parts of an urban legend. He had lived there, at the apartment building with the cats, at some point. No one could remember how long ago it had been. A few months? A few years? He had been feeding the cats while he lived there, and then he moved out, and he returned every night from wherever he lived now to make sure they still had food.

Just hotdogs though, one neighbor said.

That's right, another one said. *Never cat food.*

They seemed excited to talk to me, pleased to have useful information.

One neighbor told me that the Hotdog Man hadn't left the cats willingly; he had been evicted. Another said that when he lived there, he had left his apartment door open all the time so that all thirty cats could come and go as they pleased. The first neighbor shrugged and said: *That's probably why he was evicted.*

The cats were sickly and thin, with the dull look cats get when all their energy is focused on survival. They weren't friendly; they would scatter if I got too close. There were a lot of kittens. There were a lot of postpartum female cats, their nipples distended, a sign that they had palm-size kittens hidden somewhere we would have to find. The cats weren't starving—they were eating hotdogs, seemingly endless amounts of them—but they didn't look good.

He drives a gold Mustang, one neighbor told me. *He comes every night with hotdogs and milk.*

That first night there I stayed as late as I could, hoping to run into the Hotdog Man. I wanted to let him know that I could help with the cats, that I could get them all spayed and neutered before there were more of them. I wanted to offer him cat food. I wanted to thank him for caring about the cats, enough that he drove there every night. I wanted to ask him: *Why hotdogs?*

But by midnight there was no sign of him. I left my big bowls of cat food and fresh water and a note for him, introducing myself and thanking him and offering help, with my phone number and a smiley face and a little drawing of a cat, and when I went back in the morning the note was gone and the ground was covered in hotdogs.

I'VE SEEN STRAY CATS EATING dog food, cats eating fish food, cats gnawing on pizza crusts. Cats licking sloppy mounds of baked beans, cats slurping vegetable lo mein from a take-out container, backing up their whole bodies to pull out the long dangling noodles. I've seen cats eating french fries, cats eating old lettuce, cats eating lamb curry. Cats eating potato salad, a huge tray of it, the gloppy mayonnaise sitting all day in the Arizona sun. My stomach bubbling at the smell of it.

More people than you realize are walking to the dollar store to buy the cheapest pasta they can find, are boiling it and draining it and mixing it with kibble, with old deli meat, with whatever will make the food go further. Putting it out in big trays for the stray cats living in their backyards, in their driveways, on their front porches, the cats roaming their trailer parks and apartment complexes and strip malls, the cats that emerged from under their shed one spring and then never went away. The cats they never meant to care for; the cats they can't afford but are still trying to. The cats, still hungry. The cats, still reproducing because they've never been to a vet.

All the imperfect ways we show up for small animals. So what if the cats were eating nothing but hotdogs? I had seen much hungrier cats.

I TRAPPED TEN OF THE CATS outside Taylor's building and started naming them hotdog-related names. Frank, Ketchup, Footlong. Taylor's apartment building shared a chain-link fence with an abandoned lot next door, and that's where the cats were coming from; I would drive up at dusk and the lot would look empty at first, just old trash and scrubby brush, until I focused my eyes through the holes in the fence and really stared. Most of the cats were dusty brown tabbies and they blended in with the dirt until they moved.

Taylor had started feeding them every night at six, big heaping bowls of cat food, and then twelve hours later, every single morning, picking up the hotdogs that would appear overnight. By the time she got to the hotdogs they would have little bite marks in them; they'd be gnawed-on and slimy, coated in dirt like powdered donuts from the way the cats pawed them around.

I was still trying to meet the Hotdog Man. I wanted to establish myself as a friendly presence; I wanted to at least make sure he knew we weren't harming the cats. When he showed up now in the black of night to feed his cats, he would find some of them with freshly shaved bellies, new incisions, new ear tips showing they were spayed. I was still leaving notes. *Thank you for feeding the cats here! We are getting them spayed/neutered. We will not harm them.* I kept leaving my phone number.

Every time my phone rang, I answered. Every time I hung up Tim would look at me and say: *Was that spam again? Why do you keep answering spam calls?*

I looked at him like it was obvious. I said: *I thought it might be the Hotdog Man.*

I was bringing volunteers with me to help trap the cats so we could spread out in pairs, setting traps in Taylor's yard and the empty lot next door and in the alley that ran behind the property. It was a neighborhood with a lot of foot traffic and not all of it friendly. Each night before setting our traps I would gather the volunteers into a little huddle, lay out the game plan, remind everyone to stay with a buddy and bring a flashlight and grab me if they needed help. And I would remind them: *Keep an eye out for a gold Mustang. That's the Hotdog Man.*

THERE'S AN ELDERLY MAN WHO leaves an entire boiled chicken each night for the stray cats that live in his shed. I spent weeks trying to convince him to pull the chicken off the bones first, to leave just the meat for the cats. *They like it this way*, he kept saying, adding another full steaming chicken with its weird puckered skin to the pile of chicken bones in the corner of the shed.

And then one of the cats started hacking, acting weird, pawing at his mouth, and after several days of refusing to eat finally climbed into a trap so I could take him to the vet, and upon sedated examination was found to have a whole chicken bone, soft and splintering, stuck across the roof of his mouth. I tried explaining to the man: cats shouldn't have access to the bones like that; this could have ended much worse. *This is how they like it!* he kept saying, and he was getting both angry and teary-eyed. *You're acting like I don't care about these cats.*

I could picture him: every day that hot summer, the steam rising from the chicken boiling on his stove. The price of a whole chicken. His careful navigating, the tennis balls on the bottom of his walker, across the yard to the shed; the cats gathering around him; how gently he lowered another day's chicken to the ground. How he'd go without food if he needed to, to afford it. His joy watching the cats tear off strips of meat. His devotion.

He said it again: *You're acting like I don't care about these cats.*

ONE OF THE NEIGHBORS TOLD US that the Hotdog Man mostly spoke Spanish. I took down my notes. Translated them to Spanish. Put them back up.

Maybe he can't read? the neighbor said.

I wanted to talk to the Hotdog Man because his cooperation could help us catch the remainder of the cats, and because the hotdogs he was leaving every night were starting to cause health issues for the cats, and because I wanted him to know that someone else cared. That they were getting real food now, that Taylor was always looking out for them, that he could call me any time. That he didn't have to do it alone.

There was something about the hotdog cats that reminded me of my own: maybe just that there were thirty of them, or that Taylor was also a young woman who cared about cats but had no idea how to help them, or that the cats needed better care than they were getting even though everyone was trying their best. It was meaningful to me to think about what I would have done differently if I had inherited my cats with the resources and knowledge I had now, and then to do those things for the hotdog cats, to be able to jump in and help Taylor the way I wish I had been helped.

On my first visit there I loaded my car with donated cat food, stainless-steel bowls, cat trees, and scratchers. I showed up with my traps and I took ten cats and I came back with the same cats but healthier and happier, and all of it was free. I was imagining what it could have been like for me if someone had shown up at my house that way, had said: *I know it's weird to suddenly have thirty cats, but believe it or not there are a lot of us. There are a lot of us who care.*

Maybe I found myself relating to the Hotdog Man, too. I didn't know anything about him. But I had spent enough nights in my driveway feeding my cats whatever I could afford, feeling like their sole protector, the only person who could love them correctly. He cared enough about these cats that he drove there every night, in any weather, presumably after every kind of workday. He never missed a night. Did he buy his hotdogs every day? Did he have a fridge full of them? Surely he felt alone in his dedication to the cats. Surely he knew that the neighbors thought he was a little crazy. That's all I really wanted to tell him: that I didn't think he was crazy.

I get it, I wanted to tell him. *There are a lot of us who care.*

———

MY WORK LIES SOMEWHERE in the dissonance between what animals need from us and what we want to give them, the tension between wanting to help cats and wanting to *feel* like we're helping cats. Helping cats in the way we imagine they need help, helping cats in a way that makes us feel good. Going to bed at night patting ourselves on the back, knowing the cats are fed, while outside the door the cats are circling a bowl of milk they can't digest, an old chicken that will make them sick. A pasta salad that will leave them oily and malnourished.

In all my early days in our driveway I had given the cats toys and treats: little plastic balls, dangling ribbons, liquid treats I squeezed from a pouch right into the cats' waiting mouths. I had sewn toys for them myself, wrapping catnip into scraps of fabric. I had spent all my hours with them; I had cried desperate tears when I didn't know what else to do.

The first time I met another rescuer, the first person who showed me how to use a trap, she told me I wasn't doing enough. She told me I needed more water bowls, I was feeding them the wrong food, I hadn't taken them to the vet. She told me I didn't care about them. Me, awake all night with the cats, chasing them from the street, counting them every hour to make sure they were all still alive. *Clearly,* she had said, *you don't care about these cats.*

I TRIED AGAIN TO STAY late at Taylor's apartment to watch for the Hotdog Man. I didn't know what time he'd come but I knew he'd be there. He never missed a night.

It had been six weeks by then, since my first reconnaissance mission to Taylor's building, and the Hotdog Man had to have noticed the changes. He had to have noticed the bowls of cat food Taylor was putting out every evening, the clean water every morning, the cat trees. He had to have noticed that all the cats with crusty faces were clear-eyed now, the antibiotics they had gotten at the vet finally kicking in. Did he notice there were no new kittens? Did he know what the ear tips meant? They were incremental, the changes, but it was hard to miss how good the cats were starting to look by then.

He was still leaving hotdogs.

That night I could hear his car before I saw it. Taylor was with me, waiting for the Hotdog Man, and she heard it first. *That's a Mustang*, she said, and we both looked up at the driveway, waiting to see if it was gold. The cats had heard the car too. They were gathering, shimmying out of their hiding places, appearing suddenly from every direction.

It seemed ridiculous that we had been spending our nights trying to trap the last five stubborn cats with cat food and tuna and rotisserie chicken, waiting for hours in the dark, trying to figure out where they were hiding, when there was one simple thing that could draw them out in an instant: the Hotdog Man.

The Mustang was gold. It pulled halfway into the driveway and Taylor and I started to stand, smiling, trying to look approachable. I was always trying to send a silent signal from my mind, a telepathic message: *We love cats, too! We're not here to harm them!*

The cats lined up along the side of the driveway. The Hotdog Man saw us.

He put the car in reverse, backed out of the driveway, and sped away. We could hear his car leaving the neighborhood, getting farther and farther away.

Does he think he's in trouble? Taylor said.

I shook my head. Did he know we had been picking up his hotdogs every morning and throwing them away? Did he think we were there to chastise him?

The cats were confused, looking around at each other and then back to the street, wondering where the car they recognized had gone. I refilled their food bowls and put out some treats, but they ignored me. They wanted the Hotdog Man.

———

ONE WOMAN, UNABLE TO AFFORD vet care and unsure how to cure the red circles of ringworm that kept appearing on the stray cats she fed, tried Vicks VapoRub. *They don't really let me touch them*, she told me. *But I sneak up on them while they're eating and slap a glob on them.*

Has that been working? I asked her.

No, she said, and she didn't elaborate.

I'm fascinated by people's interpretations of care, their motivations, the lengths they go to. The things they try. Sometimes it's desperation, the best effort they can afford. The leftovers, the old pizza crusts, the attempts at vet care without going to a vet. Sometimes it's not knowing better. The gulf between the care we want to give and the care we have access to.

I like to catalog every misguided effort, every strange offering:

woman will only feed dog food to cats; man gave kitten oat milk; woman convinced mayonnaise is good for cats' fur; woman tried using Italian dressing on cat to treat fleas; woman knits handmade beds for cats but doesn't believe in getting cats spayed; woman has been baking pound cake specifically for feral cats; man won't stop leaving saucers of milk by the dumpster; cats are eating leftover egg rolls; cats are eating boiled onions; cats are eating moldy cereal; woman wants to try human cold medicine before bringing injured cat to the vet; man works at ice cream shop and brings home whipped cream for cats; woman cooks daily scrambled eggs for cats; man has been driving across town to scatter hotdogs along the street for cats, every single night, possibly for years.

———

ONE MORNING I GOT A TEXT from Taylor. It said: *I just met the Hotdog Man.*

I texted back: *!!!!*

I figured she had been out late and had run into him, scattering his hotdogs in the dirt outside her apartment. Her text gave no indication of how the interaction had gone, whether he was scared of her or grateful for her or angry with her. From what we could gather from neighbors, the Hotdog Man seemed to consider all thirty of the cats his own, and I wouldn't have been surprised to learn that he was angry at us for intervening in their care. Maybe he had seen the hotdogs in the trash. *We've been trying to connect with you*, I was already saying in my head, preparing my response in case he was mad.

Give him my phone number, I was ready to tell Taylor. *I will deal with it.*

But Taylor's next text said: *He came to my door. He wanted to say thanks.*

On my second night trapping cats in Taylor's yard, I had accidentally left some scraps of old sheets behind. I had been using them to cover the traps as we caught cats; it keeps the cats calm. The sheets were ancient, threadbare, cut into scraps; they couldn't have provided more than a quarter-inch of cushion. But the next morning there were cats sleeping on them.

In the weeks after that I brought cat beds, the plushest ones I could find, and lined them up along Taylor's building where the overhang of the roof protected them from the weather. The cats piled into the beds. We named two cats Mustard and Relish and they shared a bed every night, their little paws wrapped around each other. A big orange cat I had named Oscar Mayer had claimed the softest bed, the one shaped like a big bucket, with six inches of memory foam under him. He blinked his contentment.

The Hotdog Man had seen the beds. That's what did it for him. Not the vet care, not the big bowls of food. Not the fact that the cats were looking shinier by then, were filling out from having access to real cat food. It was the beds, the whole line of them, each one overflowing with piles of cats curled up together, that convinced him to trust us.

He had tears in his eyes, Taylor texted me. *His name is Francisco.*

BY NOW I'M USED TO the angry emojis in my social media comments. It can be hard not to react with anger to the people I mention in my captions, the people I write about in the cat stories I share. The people who have been feeding stray cats for years but never got them spayed or neutered, the people whose attempts at feeding cats make the cats sick, the people who don't bring injured cats to the vet in time. All the accidental suffering.

How could anyone be so awful?! the comments say. So awful, so stupid, so uncaring. *How could they not care?*

Can we hold empathy for people whose attempts at care accidentally cause harm? In all my creeping around alleys, all my crawling under the skirting of mobile homes, all the notes I've left on dumpsters and water bowls and cat beds, I've seen people stretching their budgets, staying up late, sharing the last of the food in their fridge with the stray cat waiting on their front step. People crafting cat beds, driving across town, walking the streets in bad weather with backpacks full of cat food. The notes they write back to me, the scrawled handwriting, the strange, silly efforts at loving cats: I can't bring myself to begrudge them. I've seen such extraordinary attempts at care.

LEARNING THE HOTDOG MAN'S NAME was like getting a clear photo of Bigfoot. Francisco. I couldn't believe Taylor had met him without me. I bugged her with questions. How late at night did he come? How long had he been feeding the cats? Why the hotdogs?

Taylor shrugged. She said: *It kinda looked like he's living out of his car.*

The gold Mustang. I pictured it full of everything he owned, a whole life in a little car. Is that why he hadn't taken any of the cats with him when he moved?

I think a few of the cats were his pets, Taylor said, *and he had to leave them behind.*

It was a common way cat colonies formed. A few abandoned cats, if not fixed, could turn into thirty in under a year. I wondered what it was like for Francisco to come back every night and see his beloved pets slinking through the dark, the cats he couldn't keep with him in his car. To watch them turn into more cats, dozens more cats, all of them increasingly hungry, increasingly desperate, Francisco in his gold Mustang doing everything he could. I wanted to know how many hotdogs he bought at a time.

ONE MORNING TAYLOR GOT UP and there were no hotdogs on the ground. The cats didn't seem to care. They had grown less and less interested in the hotdogs as they had gotten used to the steady supply of cat food every evening; most mornings the hotdogs were untouched. The cats stayed in their beds.

The Hotdog Man—Francisco, now—came back the next night, and the night after that. Just a fluke that he had had to take a night off.

Taylor started to see him around more. Sometimes he left notes, scrawled in big scratchy handwriting. *NO PHONE*, one of them said. Taylor sent me a picture of it.

He doesn't have a phone, she wrote. *That's why he's never called.*

By then we had gotten all thirty cats to the vet; there were no new kittens and no new diseases spreading rampant among them. We had started assembling straw-filled shelters for them as the weather cooled. Taylor was diligent, putting out fresh water every morning and food every night. I bought hotdog-themed cat toys, little fabric corndogs and ketchup packets. I wondered if Francisco ever noticed them on the ground. If he found them charming.

The night I finally met him I didn't mean to. I wasn't trapping cats; I wasn't waiting late for him. I was dropping off another week's worth of cat food for Taylor when I heard his engine approaching. He was early that night. The cats perked up at the sound of his car.

The gold Mustang parked in the driveway that used to be his. His old apartment was still vacant. Sometimes it seemed like no one would care if he just stayed, if he moved right back in with the cats. One of the neighbors had shaken his head when I said this out loud. *He comes at night because the landlord keeps telling him to stay off the property*, he said. *Because of the cats.*

Francisco stayed in his car for a minute, behind deeply tinted windows, and I wondered if he was avoiding me. If he was going to turn around and leave. When he cut the ignition and stepped out, I realized what he had been doing. He was opening an eight-pack of hotdogs.

Francisco, I said, approaching him. It felt strange to say his name, strange to see him in person after months of imagining a faceless man in a gold car throwing hotdogs out the window. He somehow looked exactly as I had pictured him. Friendlier, maybe. He had a wide, gleeful grin.

Ah, he said, holding his hand out to shake mine. *I have been hearing about you.*

I wondered what the neighbors told each other about me. The woman catching cats in big metal cages, throwing away their hotdogs, dumping out their milk. Bringing hotdog-themed toys, like it was all a joke. The woman waiting for the guy in the gold Mustang.

There was a language barrier between me and Francisco. He was mostly gesturing at the cats and smiling, clasping his hands together in thanks, waving around his package of hotdogs. I wanted to ask him everything. I wanted to know the entire progression of his life, everything that had ever happened to lead him here. He had left his driver's-side door open, and I was trying not to be weird about it, looking inside at his things, but I kept stealing glances as he crouched to pet the cats. I was trying to absorb as much information about him as I could.

He was wearing a broad hat. He was with a black cat—one of the cats that had been his pet originally—and he was tipping the package of hotdogs so that the liquid from it dripped directly into the cat's mouth. I realized that the eight-pack of hotdogs he was holding was already missing one. He hadn't only been opening the package in his car. He had been eating one.

When I told Taylor later, she nodded. *I thought that's what he was doing*, she said. *I think it's his dinner every night and then he gives the rest to the cats.*

The hotdogs were inscrutable to me. Francisco knew by then that the cats weren't eating the hotdogs, that they didn't need the hotdogs, that they barely even liked the hotdogs. That it would be better for everyone if he didn't leave the hotdogs. That he was making more work for me by leaving the hotdogs, that I would pick them up as soon as he left. But he couldn't stop smiling with all the cats around him, the way they reached their paws up his legs and stretched. It wasn't a chore to him, and he didn't want to be relieved of it. It was a demonstration of care that was foreign to me—hotdogs as offering, hotdogs as ritual, hotdogs as care—but it mattered to him.

I made one more offering of my own: a bulk-size tub of cat treats for Francisco if he wanted them. I knew the cats loved them; I left a few for them every time I was there. He shook his head in an exaggerated way, like I had done way too much already, like he couldn't possibly accept.

No, no, he said, laughing, his grin so much wider than I could have imagined it being, *it is my pleasure*. And then, like he had never been so thrilled to do anything in his life, he shook his hotdogs into his hands, tore them up into chunks, and threw them in the air like confetti.

The Pigeon House

We called it the Pigeon House because it was full of them.

Hundreds of pigeons were living in the yard and the shed and the greenhouse, roosting and swooping and cooing, the ground powdery with decades of dried droppings, the air downy with feathers. It was hard to breathe. It was hard to walk: the yard was piled with trash and old clothes, rotting cardboard and rubble, old furniture long since molded over. It was dark out and we were finding our footing by feel, trying to find something solid under each step. I couldn't figure out the texture under my feet, both crunchy and plush, both velvet and wet.

I crouched with a flashlight.

It was pigeons. It was dead pigeons, in every stage of decomposition.

The ground is corpses, the girl next to me said, and I nodded. It was.

I was at the Pigeon House because it was also full of cats. The property had been condemned by the city and the homeowner was being evicted and the house was swarming with cats about to be left behind. They were living in the rubble, giving birth under layers of feathers, fighting all night over birds.

There were at least forty cats in the yard and more trapped inside the house. No one knew how many. From the yard I could see their nose prints pressed against the windows.

The homeowner was named Sharon, and she was crying, standing at the open front door, blocking my view inside. She warned me: things had gotten out of control. She hadn't been able to keep up with cleaning. She didn't know how this had happened.

The cats, she said. *They've started shitting everywhere.*

I know, I told her.

I did know. I knew because I had done this before. I knew because there was nothing less surprising she could have said.

This was the eighth animal-hoarding situation I had responded to and in some ways they had started to feel less shocking. People lived like this. It was a fact I had learned quickly in all my work with cats, a reality I had already integrated into my understanding of the world. The details change: the things people collect, the condition of the house, the number of animals—but in each case I was left with the same core feeling when I got home, like I had gotten very lucky in life without ever even realizing what I had avoided. At my first hoarding situation the cats were draped across the inside of a mobile home, all of them limp, and I had to climb over piles of trash to check each cat, to see which ones were still alive. In my second, the trailer caught fire and burned down before I could go back. All the cats were still inside.

I was still an amateur when I arrived at the Pigeon House, but I felt like I was hard to shock. *Try me*, I wanted to say to Sharon, and she finally let me into her house, unlocked the gate to the backyard, and I stepped inside.

WE HAD MOVED IN TO the brick house in Poets Square knowing we would someday move out. It was how I had moved in to every place I had lived: keeping things in storage, ignoring the small repairs that could make the place nicer. They weren't my problem. I was just passing through.

It was a rental, and we had planned to only stay a year. Maybe two. We were saving up, we said, to buy a house someday, although the realities of our finances and the housing market made that less likely than we wanted to admit. Saving what? Neither of us had any extra money left over after bills each month. I didn't even know my own credit score. Buying a house was less of a real goal and more of a daydream, the kind of thing we had both told ourselves for years when rent went up again, when neighbors were loud, when landlords ignored termites and roof leaks.

The house in Poets Square: it was just another way station, a little layover on our way to a more permanent life.

We hadn't planned on the cats. We couldn't have known that over the course of our first year there our covered carport would turn into a feral cat sanctuary, a full buffet of cat foods every night, heated cat beds, fresh water. That the eaves of our roof would be full of cats, that the back patio would be taken over by cats, that the bushes on the south side of the property would be home to so many cats. That we would meet our neighbors. That we would like it there.

After a year in Poets Square, I had started to get anxious when I thought about moving again, about ever affording another place to live, about ever living somewhere stable and safe where no one could take it all away from me. About what would happen to the cats if we left. There were still fourteen of them living there, all the more feral ones who couldn't be adopted or relocated. There was no version of my life where I would ever leave the cats behind. We'd just keep signing yearlong leases, we agreed. We'd stay awhile.

It was April of our second year there when our landlord asked if we could talk. She was selling the house. We would need to leave.

I'm not trying to force you onto the streets, she said. *But I'm motivated to sell.*

Tim was worried about money—he was always worried about money—but I was worried about the cats, the idea of moving, the logistics of it, my mental health, my entire sense of safety and surefootedness in the world. I hadn't meant to build a life in Poets Square. I hadn't realized what it meant to me. All the sweet things: the risotto Tim would make, the glow-in-the-dark stars, the exact spot in the driveway where I sat each night with the cats.

We looked for new places. Places that allowed dogs. Places that allowed cats. Places that allowed feral cats, fourteen of them. Places close enough to Poets Square that I could walk back each night and check on the cats there. I hadn't realized how low our rent was; apartments much worse than our house were more than we could afford. I wondered if I could convince the landlord to include a provision about the cats when the house sold. I wondered who I would be if I didn't live there, if I didn't sit in the driveway, if I didn't have over a dozen cats. Could I refuse to leave? I was looking up laws about tenants' rights, trying to buy as much time as I could.

The landlord was scheduling appraisals, getting ready for showings.

It stretched on for weeks, the stress of it, and I woke every morning with my mouth bloody from chewing the insides of my cheeks. We started looking into buying the house—I had sent a panicked message to our landlord asking if she'd be willing to sell directly to us so we could stay—and the numbers that came back from mortgage lenders were much larger than I expected. I had only just begun making money from social media and even if we drained our savings to make the minimum down payment, the monthly mortgage would be too high. Every day we were looking at long columns of numbers, interest rates, utility statements. The numbers were tens of thousands of dollars short.

Do you have family who could help with a down payment? our lender was asking us. *Any upcoming bonuses from work? Savings you can tap into?*

I had medical debt and fourteen cats. I had come to think of them as my own.

It was a last-ditch effort when I shared a link to a GoFundMe online. I had shared the situation on Instagram and TikTok because I was stressed and not posting my regular cat content because of it. How was I supposed to tell all my followers, my whole online community, that I would have to leave the house that started everything? That I would have to leave the cats? I tried to be frank in my post: *I don't know yet what we're going to do.*

My followers acted instantly. They begged: *Could you start a fundraiser? Would you let us help?*

It didn't seem like a bad idea. If we could crowdfund a bit of money for closing costs, and if Tim worked overtime and I got a second job, and we worked ourselves to the bone for many years to come, we might be able to pull it off. I made a fundraiser. I shared the link.

And then, in four hours, we raised $50,000.

I watched the donations roll in and the total number tick up, one dollar after another, and I sat stunned, knowing I should be thanking each person individually but instead just frozen there, soaking in a feeling I couldn't name. It was gratitude and disbelief, and it was discomfort, and it was relief like I had never known before, a relaxing of a muscle I didn't know I had been clenching. My whole life, scraping together rent. My whole life, wondering where I'd go next.

Tim, I said. He had been pulling out patches of his beard, poring over numbers. He looked up.

We have fifty thousand dollars, I told him. He stared at me.

We can buy the house, I told him.

We can stay here, I told him.

We sat up all night in squirmy disbelief, feeling itchy with possibility, squeezing each other's hands. When Tim finally went to bed, I did what I did every night: I went outside and sat in the driveway in the dark, just me and the cats and the quiet, and I tossed them treats and I marveled at their smallness, at how little they knew.

We're staying here, I whispered to Monkey, and she flopped over on her side in response.

Because of you, I told her, and she rolled over, baring her white belly. She was one of the first cats we had found in the driveway, one of the first cats who kept me up at night worrying, and all of that—those two years of love and stress, vet bills and worry, two years of sitting in that same spot in the driveway every morning and every night, cross-legged with the cats just out of reach—all of that was suddenly wrapped up in that one moment, with Monkey's belly in the air and the house around us about to be our own.

In the distance, in the dark, I could see Sad Boy and Lola sitting on the roof, MK walking across the hood of my car, François coming toward me for treats. Georgie was chasing a moth.

We're staying here, I whispered to all of them, wanting them to understand, and they moved through the darkness with just their eyes lit up, reflecting back at me.

SHARON WAS ASHAMED OF the state of her house. She was ashamed of all of it: the pigeons, the cats, the way her life had gone. *This isn't who I am*, she kept saying.

I believed her. By then I had seen plenty of properties and lives gone off course, and each of them was uniquely tragic, these little glimpses into how a life can spiral. Most of the cases I worked were in low-income neighborhoods, in mobile home parks and apartment complexes and alleys. Behind businesses, near dumpsters. They were people living in poverty. They were people who had been living in poverty for a long time, and often in their homes you could see their whole lives laid out before you in piles and stacks: a couch yellowed with age, a roof leak at least a decade old, the stains there so long they were permanent. The piles of garbage rotted together so long ago that they had taken new forms, had turned into new types of garbage. I felt heavy and intrusive in these places, witnessing the private detritus of lives held together by a thread.

The Pigeon House was huge, on an enormous property in a wealthy neighborhood, and although it was in disrepair, I could tell it had once been a spectacular house. The backyard led to a second backyard, where a guesthouse was falling down next to an old greenhouse. There was a pond. A shady patio with French doors leading into the house. A shed full of an old art collection, the pieces molded over and crumbling. Roaches crawling out from under everything. The pigeons.

There were plants everywhere, overgrown in colorful glazed pots. There were twinkling lights strung up along the house, stretching out over what must have been a garden, vines tugging them down.

I could look at that yard, the ground feathered and buzzing with flies, the piles of trash tipping over into each other, the cats starving and staring, darting between overgrown patches of grass, and I could imagine it like a photo overlay of what it had once been: a place for garden parties, a little sanctuary of greenery and birds, a place where someone had meticulously tended the garden and sat in the early morning with coffee, waking up with the day.

It was the kind of property I had always wished I owned. It was somehow still nicer than anything I'd ever be able to afford. I found myself clearing piles of garbage and pigeon droppings, pushing aside dead animals to get to the ones still living, breaking back dead branches to push through broken windows and holding my breath even behind my respirator, and feeling the most bizarre sense of jealousy. Of bitterness. Of thinking: *There are people who would die to ever live somewhere like this, and this is what has become of it.*

Sharon was crying. Sharon was apologizing. *It's okay*, I kept telling her, although I couldn't tell if I meant it. It wasn't okay, the way animals were suffering. It wasn't okay that she was living like this among them. At that moment, before the GoFundMe, I didn't know where I would be living by the following week. I wanted a backyard and a greenhouse and an art collection, a patio with blue pots and twinkling lights. I wanted to build a life and keep it.

Sharon wanted to tell me her story. Part of me wanted to listen. I was there for the cats, but part of my work was always about people, listening to them, witnessing all the ways they had been failed. Part of me needed Sharon to just let me work. There were bulldozers coming in two days and the piles of rubble were still full of crying kittens.

There was a team of us there and we took turns consoling Sharon, distracting Sharon, letting her talk. She told each of us a different version of her story. She had been caring for her disabled mother for eight years. She had been abandoned by her family, she had gotten behind on bills. She couldn't keep up with the property. She didn't know where the cats had come from. She loved the cats. She hated the cats. She walked with a limp, but she couldn't remember why. She didn't know yet where she would go. She would live in her car. She didn't have cats here. No, there were no cats. She had never seen a cat before. The pigeons? No, she didn't know anything about pigeons.

I tried to imagine Sharon a decade earlier, Sharon if whatever had happened to her hadn't happened. If whatever version of her story was true hadn't been. *I've been trying to get help*, she kept saying, and I believed her. I imagined it: Sharon with friends who helped tend to the yard, Sharon with family who helped care for her mother, Sharon with any kind of safety net that stepped in when she struggled. Sharon with access to mental health care. Sharon tending her garden, refilling a birdfeeder, reading a book on her patio with the dappled sunlight filtering through the trees.

I'm trying my best, she said, and then she sat down, right there in the yard, in a way that made me think she was never going to get up again.

We spent all night digging kittens out of rubble. The yard stretched on, the pigeons decomposing, the smell unbearable, the string lights twinkling above us. *This place used to be beautiful*, the lights said. So many of the world's worst tragedies aren't making headlines. They're just here, in backyards, quietly rotting away.

THE FIRST THING I DID when I learned that we'd be able to buy the house in Poets Square was sit down in our backyard and imagine. It was early spring and everything was dead: the grass brown, the bougainvillea ant-eaten. I hadn't been watering anything. It didn't matter.

It was a luxury to imagine: the grass green and cleanly mowed, the flowering vines reaching tendrils toward the sky. Colorful glazed planters, the expensive kind that I coveted in all our neighbors' gardens. The kind of life I could have here.

I had never thought before to imagine a future. To plan for it. I spent my twenties so severely depressed, feeling so at odds with the world, that it never occurred to me that I could survive it. I never meant to live past thirty.

I was seventeen when I fell into my first depressive episode, and it happened like flipping a switch: one day my brain worked and the next it simply didn't. I couldn't feel a thing; I couldn't remember what a single emotion felt like. I stopped eating. I stayed up late tracing the veins that ran along my wrist and doing nothing about it.

Depression was physically painful for me, left me clawing at myself, and when I got overwhelmed I would lie face down on the floor, spread-eagle, like life could pass right over me if I could keep myself flat enough. At some point in my twenties a doctor had told me that I was already on the maximum dose of antidepressants, that there was nothing left to try, and although I would learn later that this was wrong, it colored how I thought of myself for a long time: as a lost cause. It became part of who I was, an identity I took no steps to heal. It was core to me, my sadness.

I moved to Tucson to escape myself, moved apartments every year, collected and threw away cheap furniture from Facebook Marketplace. I was reckless with my life, reckless with the care of people who loved me. What did it matter?

And then at some point I accidentally survived.

That dry spring in the house that was now ours, we bought a hose and a sprinkler and a watering can and I became obsessive about it, watering the yard in the early mornings while the cats ate breakfast, cleaning in the evenings as the sun went down, tearing down dead vines and hauling piles of brush to the curb. I examined each new leaf on every plant, every new tendril from our flowering vines, looking constantly for confirmation that things were growing. That things could thrive here.

The cats watched from the roof, from their perches along the wall, from their cat towers on the patio, eyeing me sleepily as I brought out garden shears and fertilizer, scattering as I hauled out the hose. The yard was always littered with cat toys, and it became part of my routine to pick them up each morning, to return them to a little basket on the patio and then watch as Lola chased the toys back into the yard, picking them up between her paws and tossing them in the air. The bougainvillea was flowering again, magenta and lush, and as the days got hotter Georgie would slip in between the branches and nap in their shade, and I'd find her later with petals in her fur.

You're the kind of person who grows flowers, I would tell myself, feeling wholly disconnected from whatever version of myself had once wanted to die. *You're buying this house. You wake up early to care for the cats who live in your garden. You're alive, you're alive, you're alive.*

INSIDE THE PIGEON HOUSE, the kitchen counters were butcher block, the backsplash blue tile.

I focused on those details because they kept me grounded, kept me from processing anything else.

That wasn't that bad, I remember thinking, driving home that first night.

I can't believe how bad that was, I remember thinking the next morning.

We went back the next night and I stood there in the kitchen, cats scurrying through their own shit at my feet, their ribs showing and their eyes dull, and I thought: *I don't feel anything about this at all.* The air was hazy with smells. There was stained glass in the window. There was a painting of butterflies.

The team of us working inside the house kept our eyes down, kept quiet, worked in a kind of stunned silence. We had to use traps because the cats were too scared to grab. We had to clear paths on the floor to set a single trap. There was a bathtub in the living room, French doors stained brown, cats hiding behind every pile of trash. When we heard the noise of a trap closing, we would point, nod silently at each other, climb over piles to get to it. Hand off cats like an assembly line toward the door.

In the kitchen my brain kept ringing out in uncomfortable recognition. The way the sunset was filtering orange light into the room. The way that butterfly painting was something I would buy, something I would hang in my own home. The blue tile, the deep gorgeous hue of it, how I had always wanted butcher block in my kitchen.

IN MY TWENTIES I LIVED in an apartment where I woke up one morning to a cockroach falling on my face.

I lived in an apartment where the toilet flushed directly into the backyard. I lived in an apartment where I witnessed a murder-suicide right outside my window, and after that I stopped sleeping.

I lived in a duplex where my neighbor beat his girlfriend and she'd pound on our shared wall until I called the police, and after the police left the neighbor would pick up the potted plants on my doorstep and he'd smash them against my wall, shouting, and I'd cower inside, helpless, having no idea what to do.

I lived in a friend's spare bedroom. I lived in a communal art studio that wasn't legal to live in. I lived in that first-floor apartment with Bubbles, where the man in a red sedan followed me home from the bus stop.

It's bleak, all of it, until I think about the people who were there to move me each time, the people who kept showing up in my worst moments: my friends with trucks, my family who sent care packages to each new apartment, gaudy with colorful trinkets that looked out of place no matter where I lived. Small signs of care even when I didn't want them. All the times I thought no one would show up for me in an emergency, when actually people were already caring for me in ways I didn't recognize as care.

FOR A FEW WEEKS THIS is how I lived: spending my days in the house we now owned, in our yard, marveling at how green everything was getting, at this life that gets to be mine, and spending my evenings at the Pigeon House, suiting up in my respirator and gloves, blinking back the powdery down of pigeons, wading through rot, watching a life fall apart.

We pulled kittens out of fiberglass insulation, their heads larger than they should have been, their proportions grotesque. We pulled kittens from swarming nests of cockroaches, from moldy piles of trash, from wet leaking floors in the kitchen. There were adult cats, elderly cats, teenage cats, cats in every color. A lot of them were Siamese, their gray-blue eyes the color of pigeons, the brown stretching up their paws blending with all the filth.

We pulled forty-two cats from the Pigeon House.

The property was condemned. Sharon was evicted. Sharon was refusing to leave. Sharon was escorted off the property by cops, trying to bring cats with her, living in her car. There were rumors that the property had already been sold, that it was being bulldozed, that it would be rebuilt as an Airbnb, that it would sit exactly as it was for months.

I don't know which was true. I never went back.

In our new yard we planted a pomegranate tree, a gift from Tim's parents, in an enormous blue pot we found for free on the side of the road. It started budding, its greenness collecting into hard red beads. Tiny signs of life.

THERE TURNED OUT TO BE nothing climactic about buying our house. We already lived there. One day we were renting it and the next it was ours, and we had a mortgage for the next thirty years. I wrote a check for $50,000 and at the bank I tried to act normal about it, like it wasn't the wildest amount of money I could imagine. Like it wasn't the most enormous gift of my life.

That night I fed the cats the way I always did, the way I'd always be able to do. I felt like I had cheated something by staying, like life had been leading me toward something I had now narrowly escaped. Whatever version of my future was out there—some other apartment, some other house, leaving the cats, losing my money, being alone, going crazy, falling down someday in a yard full of pigeons, beside myself, having no idea where my life had gone, what had happened to me, who I had become—I was saved from it by a bunch of people on the internet who cared about the cats I never meant to find.

Monkey, François, MK, Georgie, I sang as I put their bowls of food out. *Sad Boy, Lola, TJ, Zippy.* New cats had started arriving that year, from other parts of the neighborhood, and with each one I added another bowl to the carport. *I'm in charge of you now*, I would tell each new cat, *and I will never let you suffer.*

At night, in the house that was now our own, I started dreaming about pigeons. The aggressive way they had flown right at my eyes when I got too near their nests. In the falling-down greenhouse in Sharon's backyard I had seen movement, small shaking creatures just barely visible in my flashlight beam. I thought they were kittens, and I reached toward them, and by the time I realized they were baby birds the pigeons were swooping at us, protecting the nest, and we were shrieking and ducking, the birds making grotesque flapping shadow shapes against the greenhouse walls.

This is like a horror movie, someone said, and it was, except it was real life. It was Sharon's life, and I was angry at all of it: the suffering, the house, the cats, the birds, everything that could have been avoided if anyone at all had cared sooner, if any systems had worked the way they should have. Some of the pigeons, we'd realize later, were domesticated. Some of them were in little cages. When I asked Sharon, she just shook her head.

You know they're not supposed to be out in the wild, right? she said, like I had asked her something ridiculous. *They need people, to survive the way they're supposed to.*

I know, I told her. She was right.

———

WHEN WE CLOSED ON THE HOUSE Tim and I stood in our kitchen clinking tiny glasses of wine. There were storm clouds gathering outside but they looked mild, yellow-pink and puffy, coloring the air. The cats were hiding, each of them in the little spaces they had claimed.

Tim was taking fresh bread out of the oven. I felt outside myself as I watched him, as I looked around our house, as I looked at the cats tucked into every corner of our yard, feeling safe and surreal.

I started noticing the pigeons all over the city, their amber eyes tracking my movements. Sharon never appeared in my dreams, or the cats. Just the pigeons, the sheer number of them, the way they flocked so closely together.

Are you doing okay? Tim asked when I started pointing out every pigeon I saw.

This is the most stable I've ever felt, I told him, and I meant it—this house, this yard, this life I never planned on living.

It's a Friday when we sign the stack of papers, when we buy the house, and that night we get rain and that weekend the yard is dewy and green, spotted with pawprints. I can recognize them by now, the different sets of prints, the hiding places they lead to. Tim and I stand outside with one arm around each other, one hand on our hips, admiring our house like proud parents. *We live here*, he says, and I'm surprised when I find myself tearing up. We have a place to live. We have people looking out for us.

We raise our plastic coffee cups in the air and touch them together with a dull noise.

To being homeowners, Tim says.

To people helping us buy a house, I say.

To cats, he says, and I nod. *To cats.*

All over the city, people are doing their best. In our little yard, I'm still alive.

An Incomplete List of Names I've Given Cats

Monster Paws
Karl Havoc
Breadstick
Disco
Eggroll
Toyota Rav4
Hot Pocket
Lobsterfest
Kevin
Turnip
Zoboomafoo
Mr. Business
Jimmy Neutron
Chaps
Baby Spice
Pigeon
Meatloaf
John Denver
Audio 2000

Tony Hawk
Party Time
Shrek
Big Thunder
Seabiscuit
Spicy Michael
Lunchbox
JPEG
Scrapyard
Trapezoid
Dunkaroo
Sponge
Banjo
Jeffrey Kisses
Shrimpy Bill
Showbiz
Cool Ranch
Flavortown
Toyotathon

An Incomplete List of Names I've Given Cats

- Strudel
- Salami
- Reduced Fat Sour Cream
- Big Cheddar
- Big Tim
- Barbara
- Derek
- Mr. Jones
- Blink-182
- Dumptruck
- Mr. Trash
- Ghost
- Noam Chomsky
- Sharky
- Feral Fawcett
- Uncle Leo
- Linguini
- Ham Boy
- Clementine
- Godzilla
- Sad Mouth Sam
- Alien
- Tropicana
- Pulp Free
- Christian Dior
- Feral Gerald
- Jetpack
- Coleslaw
- Ramona Quimby
- Doppler Radar
- Weasel
- Stilton
- Fig Jam
- Trader Joe
- Wizard
- The Mayor
- Dinky
- Lola
- Baby Paws
- Kool-Aid Man
- Ballpark Frank
- Lou Bega
- Mambo #5
- Reverse Monkey
- Egg
- Gale Force Winds
- Surf and Turf
- Rump Roast
- Tomasito
- Crunchwrap Supreme
- Jumble
- Big Daddy Havarti
- Diet Coke
- Monkey
- Shovel
- Long John
- Cow
- Yukon Gold Potato
- Mr. Ears

Acknowledgments

This book is a product of thousands of people who have loved me, supported me, advocated for me, educated me, consoled me, and rallied around me.

Thank you:

To my agent Caroline Eisenmann, who saw the promise in this project from the first thirty cats, and to my editors Libby Burton and Helen Garnons-Williams, who have championed this book the whole way. To everyone at Crown and Fig Tree who worked on this book.

My thanks to my team at Fig Tree in the UK: Ella Harold, Annie Lucas, Natalie Chapman, Sabeehah Saleq, Leah Boulton, Charlotte Faber and Josie Staveley-Taylor.

To Kati Standefer for taking my call, to Melissa Goodrich for all the early drafts, and to Robin Garabedian for knowing way back in the day that it would all happen (and for always sending pictures of cute dogs).

To my teachers Dr. Kerop Kenneth "Doc" Chakemian and Bill Bourbeau.

To Ian Williams: my heart. None of it would have happened without you.

To Sam Buck, who has celebrated my success as if it were her own.

To Kieran Carney, for the daily texts that keep me alive.

To Ethan Myerson and Keri Dixon: I count you among the best people I know.

To Serena, Tiffany, Tannie, and Crystal: meeting you marked a radical shift in my life. You modeled activism, generosity, and showing up for each other in a way that changed me.

To Madison Bertenshaw, for bringing me to Tucson.

To Katy Botelho, who claimed she didn't need any more cats.

To Rose Thor, for sharing my vision of god as a feral cat.

To Maureen, for Bubbles.

To the Tucson cat crew: Angéline Fahey, MP Ibarra, Pablo Gamas, Gerald "Human Gerald" Montag III, Abby Goeller, Annie Hallett, Rachael "Lil Rachael" Milles, Scully Young, Eebee Schaefer, Alexis Ormsby-Clay, Garrett Steinbroner, Rachel Tomlinson, Lori Mares, Chelsea Powers, Shannon Partridge, Isaac Stockton, Kristen Kiernan, Stephania Falcon, Sasha Wilson, Summer Hanson, Beth Manar, Corina Valencia, Wendy McFeely, Todd and Karen Rose, Emily Barratt-Shields, and so, so many others. Team Eartip: you are the best people around.

To everyone at Santa Cruz Veterinary Clinic, the Humane Society of Southern Arizona, and Pima Animal Care Center.

To Will Zweigart and everyone at Flatbush Cats.

To the Poets Square Cats community, which has been beside me for all of this. The kind messages, the donations, the house: I could never say thank you enough.

Acknowledgments

To my parents and my family, for everything.

To Tim, who never meant to live with thirty cats. I love you.

To everyone who does TNR work, cares for community cats, fosters pets, works in animal welfare, transports rescue animals, gets resources to pet owners, organizes within their community, believes in mutual aid, keeps a can of tuna in their car, knows every emergency vet's phone number by heart, advocates for accessible vet care, stays up all night watching traps, stops to feed stray cats, shows up for each other, and believes in hope as a collective action.